Craisie Misadventures Around the World

Craisie Misadventures Around the World

Craisiedaze

Cover Art by Claire Pew

Craisiedaze Pubs

Contents

To My Family... Thank you for giving me the need and the strength to run as far away from home as possible.

To My Uncle Jim - For encouraging this book and always being there for me.

To My Mommy – The strongest person I have ever known. Thank you for loving me without limits and supporting all my craisie adventures. Not a day goes by that I don't think of you. I miss you Melen. My story, this story, is also my mother's. I wouldn't have been able to achieve what I have without her.

Introduction, Prologue, Preface...Whatever...

I have been meaning to write "my" story since I was in college. Everyone has always said...I hope you are writing a book! I always replied by saying, "I am taking notes!"

Well 30 years later I might have forgotten to take notes and therefore I have forgotten some of the stories. Much of my story won't be told in this one but you must start somewhere, and this is my beginning.

I always believe when I hear something three times in a short amount of time I have to react, and this is my reaction. The third and final call to action occurred when I was in Mexico in December 2013 with good friends telling stories as the sun set on the beach. So, what if it took a few martinis, vodka tonics, and glasses of wine to finally start?

This story is as true as my memory will make it. I have changed the names of many (but not all) to protect the guilty, and any mistakes in the stories are mine. I do tend to exaggerate and make things extra-ordinary, if you were part of the story, just enjoy the ride and be glad I didn't call you out or that I did.

My main goal for this book is to encourage young people (especially women) to go for it! Shout to the haters "I'll show you!" Work hard to accomplish your dreams, then dream again and accomplish those! Your background is your foundation, not your definition. You define yourself and you are worth it! The second goal is to demystify solo travel. Traveling by yourself, for business or personal, opens you up to new adventures.

Oh, and a NOTE – I am not a writer, I am a storyteller. I read between 20 to 30 books a month and I know a lot of authors get dinged for their "writing". I never look that deep when reading, I look at the story — is it captivating? Do I want to know what happens next? Do I believe in the characters? Feel free to judge my "writing" but I also hope you enjoy my "storytelling" because I am writing as if you are sitting with me in a room and we are swapping stories over glasses of wine. With all the, "Oh I forget a part", interruptions I am known for, especially after the second glass of wine. I have found that I am still saying it but in this case, I can go back and add it and you will never know!

Happy Reading!

1

~

Itchy Feet

To be honest "Itchy Feet" is a term I just learned recently. In my case, it's defined as the need and desire to travel and to be a part of something different. I grew up a poor white girl surrounded by diversity. My friends were from around the world. Hispanics, not just from Mexico but from El Salvador, Puerto Rico, Columbia, etc... Asians not from China and Japan but from the Philippines, Vietnam, Laos, and Cambodia. Pacific Islanders not from Hawaii but from Samoa and Tonga. And of course, African Americans.

We were poor and one of the few white families around and I was lucky to have friends who would tolerate my racist, drug addict, alcoholic stepfather. I was trying to survive him myself. I was the oldest of five (and then later six kids).

My stepfather was a drug dealer and an abuser. He beat us and our mother often. He was also racist and the meanest man I have ever met in my entire life. What sucked about him being a drug dealer was he broke rule #1 – "Don't Get High on Your Own Supply" but then again NWA didn't come out with that anthem until much later.

My mother also became a drug addict and alcoholic, mostly due to his abuse and trying to escape the pain. She was pretty awesome though. Unlike many women in her circumstance, she always put her kids first. I always felt loved and one of the ways she showed love was by the phrase "What's One More?" My stepfather wouldn't hit us if there were other people in the house so she always said "Yes" when I wanted friends to sleep over. Her response was always "Yes, what's one more?".

She was the youngest of five and always wanted a big family (which she got) and I guess to her, the comforts of home weren't material things but being surrounded by people. My mother's house was always filled with people and refugees. I remember in high school when I was away for some summer program and a friend needed a place to stay - my mom opened her house to my friend and her infant baby. She always did that. From Ronica to Trace... What's one more?

I was getting mixed signals at home. My stepfather was hateful and used derogatory names for everyone. I went to school where I was one of the few white people in my class so if I had believed half of what he was saying I wouldn't have had any friends. In retrospect, if I hadn't hated him, I might have grown up to be just like him since hate is learned. But since I despised him, I knew that he wasn't right, and I didn't believe what he said. These wonderful people opened their homes to me and showed me that "Chinese" food had different varieties (meaning different countries and cultures but it took a while for that to sink in), they invited me to cultural events and included me in their family. They loved me, protected me, encouraged me, and opened up the world to me.

In general, I don't believe in... "Should've, Could've, Would-haves" and no stronger case can be made than this. I wish my life would've been less painful, but I was blessed to be surrounded by a rich culture and diversity which probably saved my life. Many of my friends were immigrants, at least my Hispanic and Asian friends were.

My "immigrant" friends had a different mentality than other "entitled", "privileged" people (aka white folks). Their parents didn't speak English as a first language, and they were grateful to be in the US. Their parents, siblings, etc... worked two to three jobs to make sure that they not only survived but thrived. Some of them were in public housing — aka "the projects" — when we were in elementary school and middle school but by the time, we were in High School their parents owned their own house and every child of driving age had a car. Yes! Really!! And they weren't even drug dealers...This was a real example that with hard work, saving, and making good decisions, dreams can come true. Don't forget that most of them came from money in their native countries. Oftentimes, they had servants and several houses back where they came from but they chose to come to the US, most of them as refugees from wars. They had to restart, humble themselves, and take care of their family in whatever way that they could.

These families taught me so much! They taught me the value of hard work, the value of education, the value of diversity, and the value of taking care of each other. I spent most of my weekends and summers with this diverse group of people. I loved that my friend's mothers couldn't speak to me, but I would understand that "Eat By" meant "Eat Rice". Oh, and don't get me started on the food!! Having so many brothers and sisters, food went fast in our house. We never had enough, and I learned to eat fast and hide my favorites. At my friends' houses though, there always seemed to be food in their pantry even though their family was just as large as mine, if not larger. They had fruits and vegetables I had never seen before, spices that made me cry, and flavors that even to this day make my mouth water. I learned how to not only eat with chopsticks but also the joy of eating with my hands.

I would ask how to say something in Vietnamese, Tagalog, Cambodian, or Spanish and it would stay with me, and I would use it often. I learned how to count in their languages, and I knew what days were Mahjong days (and yummy new food days). I learned when to bow and when to shake hands. I celebrated Cambodian and Vietnamese New Year's, went to Quniceaneras, and watched brides change clothes at least three times during wedding receptions held in Chinese restaurants. I attended many of my friend's sibling's graduations, where they were the Valedictorians, and had a page full of scholarships. I wanted that and it motivated me and as the oldest of my family, I wanted to be that motivation for my siblings.

All of those lessons and observations, I took with me and my - not then defined "itchy feet". Little did I know that these experiences and people were shaping me into the woman I would be. I don't know where most people get their "itchy feet" but I know I got mine from the families that welcomed me into their homes and introduced me to their cultures.

2

~

My First International Experience

My first trip internationally also happened to be my first flight. It's not as exciting as it sounds though. Until right before my senior year in high school I had never been outside Kansas or Missouri. To be honest, they are interchangeable, and most people don't realize it's two states, especially when you say you are from Kansas City.

I have always enjoyed being the center of attention so of course I was always in plays etc... When I lived in Lawrence, Kansas I was a part of an original production called *T-Money and Wolf* written by a local playwright Ric Averill. It was a play about inner-city gangs and their similarity to the Nazis. I played the white girl who was friends with the girlfriend of T-Money. It won all kinds of awards, and we were chosen among many to go to Boston to perform. It was a road trip across half of America, and we had a blast! It was not only the first time many of us had left the Midwest, but it was also the first time we would see and put our feet in the ocean. Most of us were poor and family vacations were trips to see family in the next state not road trips across the country.

I think it was this trip that lit a fire in me. The next year, I traveled all over Missouri as the DECA Vice President of District 3 (mostly the suburbs of Kansas City), then to regionals in Minneapolis, Minnesota where we spent hours in the Mall of America, the largest mall in the world at the time. Then we made it to nationals in Detroit, Michigan. It was the trip to Detroit where I took my first plane ride and then the subsequent trip "internationally" to Windsor, Canada. Nothing really "funny" or "substantial" took place during this trip but I wanted to set the stage.

I did start "collecting" things on this trip. In this case, one thing I collected was menus. One specifically was collected at a Cajun place, called Fish Bones in Greektown. The waiter and I made a total production of it. He acted like he couldn't give it to me, and then secretly passed it to me behind his back. At this point in my life, I didn't feel especially attractive or influential so it was flattering that he would "play" with me. It was also the first time I ate something as exotic as alligator.

The other thing I collected was pen pals. Amazingly, every time I travel, I collect friends. Back then it was pen pals because we actually wrote letters to each other. Now, of course, we swap emails or at least become BFFs on Facebook. In this case, it was a super cute guy from somewhere and of course, we wrote for months and even exchanged our graduation tassels...so cute!

3

~

Eyes WIDE Open

In 8th grade, I decided to be an engineer. It was the fastest way to make the most amount of money in the least amount of time. I was smart and I had thought about being a lawyer or doctor, but I was tired of being poor and living on welfare, I needed instant gratification. My friends were getting pregnant and having babies, I felt like I was a mom taking care of my siblings and my mom (who was a full-blown alcoholic at the time), and I was TIRED of sleeping in a house that had cockroaches and mice!

My mom had moved us to Lawrence, Kansas after leaving my stepfather when I was 13. (BEST DIVORCE EVER!!) But I never felt right there. Where I lived in Kansas City, MO everyone was poor, so we were more or less equals; my family was a little less equal because we were such a large family but still, I never really felt discriminated against. In Lawrence though, the table had turned, and now there were all these "rich" people. They had nice clothes, and new cars at 14 (it was legal to drive in Kansas at 14 back then) and they talked differently. Hell, they even did their hair differently. I put a shout-out on Facebook that I was writing this book and one girl said to mention that I had the highest bangs in 8th grade. Well in Kansas City, that was cool, that was the style. In Lawrence, not so much.... they were going for the valley girl cheerleader, with a ponytail and ribbon look...or what's now called the "goth" look. I don't know what they called it then, but I didn't go for that! All that black with ripped stockings...not so much... so I ended up going for the cheerleader look...which again, I didn't feel comfortable with.

To try to fit in originally, I started stealing things, first clothes for myself and my family, but then I was so good that the rich white girls would ask me to steal stuff for them and they would pay me for it. Unfortunately, or fortunately, I got caught a couple of times. One time I was stealing hair spray and my sister, Maisie, was with me...HOW EMBARRASSING! She still brings it up -

"Daisie, remember when you stole that hairspray, and the guy chased you all the way down the street?"

"Yes, Maisie I do," Thanks for humbling me...again and again.

Another time was I was teaching this dumb-ass white girl how to steal, and SHE got caught but ratted me out. BITCH!!! Like I said, fortunately, I got caught. I was 13 at the time (my birthday is at the end of August so everyone was always older than me) and my probation officer would come to my school and talk to me. His name was Adonis Jordon, the point guard for the Kansas Jayhawks (he was prelaw) and at the time one of the sexiest men I would ever meet. He looked at me and said "Why" and of course I just cried. I then decided (thanks to Adonis Jordan and my sexy civics teacher (forgot his name but he was the assistant football coach too)) that I was done with stealing, but apparently not done with lying.

I was 13 years old, but I looked 16 so I lied about my age and got a job with Dairy Queen. It was hard keeping all my lies straight, but it was fun until my SSN didn't check out and I was fired. By then though I was 14 and legally able to work in Kansas so I got a job at Sonic as a carhop. I LOVED that job. Several of my friends worked there so we had a blast. I still remember the manager, Michael Mann! He was funny but demanding. I learned a lot from him including the classic "If you got time to lean you got time to clean". Around this time, since I was working, I was eating better, and I could afford my own clothes (although I had already stolen a whole wardrobe). I LOVED to work, and I loved having money coming in.

I paid $200 for my first car at 14 years old (the price of four new tires for a 1974 Pontiac Catalina) and by the time I was 15, I had three jobs and another car. I worked for the School of Engineering at KU (for $5 an hour which was more than minimum wage at the time), I worked at Sonic, and I worked at the mall selling ice cream. I was busy but I wasn't happy in Lawrence. There was too much "classism" there. I lived on the wrong street – New York (for all my hood rats!!! What What!!) Anything East of Massachusetts was considered BAD! The only thing worse would have been living in the projects- Edgewood, but since the larger apartments only had two bedrooms, my clan didn't fit. The law is two people/children per room. This really sucked though because a few of my friends lived there, and I spent most of my time there.

Other reasons I hated Lawrence were - that I had the wrong friends and boyfriends (mostly black), I was loud and obnoxious when I witnessed discrimination and honestly, I had very little patience for stupidity. In ninth grade, I protested censorship and made it to the front page of US Today (I am still looking for that online).

Back then Lawrence, for being a "college" town, was very racist. I would walk down Mass with my friends or even boyfriends and we would be heckled or jumped. One time a guy got out of his truck and yelled at me, inches from my face because I was with two black guys. He got so angry he ripped my sweatshirt almost off me. First of ALL – Neither were my boyfriends. Second of ALL – I paid for that sweatshirt and it cost me $30!! Which was a fortune back then. Needless to say, Homie Don't Play That!! No, we didn't get into a fight, these were college kids, and we were barely in high school. My boys tried to protect me but really, we just hauled our asses out of there.

For me Lawrence was too many contradictions, I was always elected leader of this and that, I got good grades, etc... but I never felt like they were there to help me and make sure I succeeded because I was a second-class citizen. My mom worked for the elementary school across the street from where we lived, and she would hear the teachers talking about how worthless the kids were and how it didn't matter what they did because they would grow up to be either drug dealers, drug addicts, or prostitutes.

This is the same school that passed my very obvious dyslexic brother but failed my very gifted brother. ARE YOU KIDDING ME??? Not too long after that, my mom transferred to a whiter, richer school. Isn't that SAD? Why do we do that to poor children? Why are teachers, not their biggest cheerleaders at this point in their life? Your mother and father DO NOT define you? YOU CAN DO IT!! Education can take you anywhere you want to be!! This is what I heard in Kansas City, where most of us were poor. Why was Lawrence different?

I think the straw that broke my back (almost literally) was when I was hit by a car by a drunk driver. I was at a high school basketball game and while crossing the street a drunk driver hit me. But of COURSE...since I was poor, I couldn't afford a good lawyer and even though this guy and his family had money - I got NOTHING!! I wasn't in a crosswalk (there is one there now) and he wasn't legally drunk (he was 0.08 but the limit was 0.1, the law now is 0.08). I first went to the ER in Lawrence, then I was life-flighted to a bigger hospital in KC where I was confined for a week. I had a head fracture that took a plastic surgeon almost 100 stitches in and out to correct, I was hit in my right leg where I still have a lump, and I walked funny for six months. Before the accident I had almost a photographic memory, I had 20/20 vision, and I was an athlete. After the accident, I couldn't concentrate (for many years) due to the pain either in my head or my back and I didn't learn as fast as I had before. My vision was now different, I needed glasses. Do you know who paid for all my bills? MY car insurance company!!! (Which I am probably still paying for.) That drunk ass bastard got away with EVERYTHING...and my future was ALMOST destroyed. I should have had at the very LEAST my college paid for, but I got nothing.

So in the middle of my junior year, I moved back to Missouri. I was tired of being a helpless poor person, who was constantly looked down upon because I didn't wear the right clothes; I had too many "ethnic" friends; and I didn't just shut up and go with the flow. I moved back because I needed residency. As I mentioned, I knew I wanted to be an engineer, and at that point, I decided I wanted to be either an aerospace or ceramics engineer and the University of Missouri-Rolla had both programs. I moved in with strangers/second cousins and enrolled myself in high school.

The Kansas City School district at this time was a "Magnet Program." As part of some desegregation policy at some time or another, this program was created. Each school would have a "theme" which they hoped would attract people of all backgrounds. My 4th and 5th grade years were spent at Tom D Korte which at the time was for "Gifted and Talented" children and then changed into an Environmental Science school. My middle school, Lincoln Middle (across the street from Lincoln High) was brand new. Lincoln Middle would be the Math and Science Magnet school and Lincoln High was College Prep. I was actually in Lincoln Middle when I moved to ass-backward Lawrence.

When I returned to KC, my top three choices were, Van Horn, the engineering school, Central, the computer science school, and Lincoln, the college prep school. I chose Van Horn because they had actual engineering classes I could take including Aerospace Engineering, CAD, Chemical Engineering, and Electronics. What was different between the time I left KC and the time I returned...was that most people didn't care about their futures, and they chose their schools based on their colors. My school colors were Red and White, so most of my classmates were Bloods.

It's funny because gangs had taken over Lawrence when I was there. What poor mothers in LA didn't know was that when they sent their babies to the Midwest to be safe, their babies started their own gangs. This again is another tale...

I did probably 80% of my education in Kansas City (I only spent about three years in Lawrence). In KC, I was a part of a lot of clubs and organizations, where teachers encouraged me, motivated me, and pushed me towards higher education. During my senior year, as a part of the KC school district, I was able to take college classes at community colleges and UMKC, and I took college-accredited classes at my high school.

My senior year in high school looked like this: I would drive from South KC to Independence to attend Calculus and Physics classes at UMKC, I would then go to my high school, have a work/study hour, attend my DECA class (which promoted marketing and entrepreneurship) and then go to my college level English class where I obtained four hours of English Lit credit. I would then head home to eat. From there I would either head to one of my three jobs or to one of my three community colleges where I was taking college-level classes.

I learned to sleep in 15-minute naps in my car during breaks. I would change into my uniforms while driving on the highway and believe it or not I still had a social life, I didn't drink, smoke, or do drugs but I LOVED to dance and KC in the early 90s was the place to be! Between E40, Tech Nine, and other local promoters, KC was the spot!! There was always some party in some warehouse where you could go and just dance. There was very minimal drinking or drugs. I know it was there, but it wasn't a part of the culture. In those days it was more about dancing and kickin' it! Yes, I saw people get killed and beat down but most of that was because some dude was talking to another dude's girl. Stupid shit! Yes, some of my friends were drug dealers, but it was a way of life and back then they were mostly selling weed. The hardest shit they sold was a joint soaked in LSD. Don't worry...I was always the sober driver.

Really though, all of these experiences just drove me harder to get into college. I had to get the fuck out of there. I loved my friends; I loved being the "whitest black girl" they had ever known but I was tired. I hated working three jobs! I hated not sleeping and I hated how my family was being treated. They were threatening my baby brother with knives and burning him with cigarettes because he was the only white boy in his class. I hated that my brothers Sean and Jimmy were alcoholics and smoking weed as early as elementary school. I hated that Maisie wanted to be anywhere else but at the house. I hated that my sister Mary Jane wanted to "have 10 kids and live on welfare".

I hated being poor and to me the only way out of this situation was education.

4

～

College

I applied to the only school I wanted to go to in September and was accepted in October. I probably applied for over 100 scholarships and received four. The best thing about being poor was that I was able to go to school on Pell Grants. God Bless whoever started that!

I went to a small engineering school in Missouri. Back then, it was called the University of MO-Rolla. It was located in Rolla, MO so the name isn't that original. It's an old school and its original and probably coolest name was Missouri School of Mines and Metrology; the mascot was a Miner and the colors were Gold and Silver!! So cool.....

It's now known as the Missouri School of Science and Technology. I could have gone to any school in Missouri or Kansas for *free,* but I had to go to the "engineering school." College was an eye-opening experience for me. I was no longer the "Smartest Person in the Room", I was now average (and in some cases below average) and trying to survive being a mere mortal in a land of gods. It took me all of one semester to admit defeat.

I was a poor white girl who thought she was black, so I did what other black women would do (and did do) in my situation, I assimilated. I wanted to join a black sorority, but they were on lockdown my freshman year because of a death the previous year. I joined a white sorority so I could not only learn to like white girls but also get help! Engineering school was no joke, white girl or not! When I started school and looked around during orientation, I could count the number of women on two hands and two feet, the number of black people on two hands, and the number of Hispanics on one hand. I realized then that I wasn't in my comfort zone. By the time I graduated the men-to-women ratio was 50:1. To put it in even more perspective, the fraternities-to-sorority ratio was 27:3, or if you like even simpler math: 7:1.

Luckily, my female fraternity, Chi Omega, liked women who fit outside the box, and they accepted me. My big sister (MBS) was Filipina and she loved dancing and hip-hop almost as much as I did. These women, who I normally would make fun of or avoid completely, accepted me, learned from me, and later supported me when I needed help with my birth sisters. Marites, her roommate Lisa, and my roommate JL were some of the most amazing women I had ever encountered. I had been born and baptized Catholic, but I had never gotten the rest of the sacraments. Their spirit, love, and peace made me want what they had, and through their encouragement, I went through RCIA my sophomore year. Marites was my sponsor, but JL and her family were my foundation. I was confirmed on Easter my sophomore year with Marites, JL, and her family, and my mom in attendance.

I don't think international travel really entered my mind in college. Not only was I just trying to survive, but I also just couldn't afford spring breaks to Cancun or skiing in Europe (or even Colorado). Hell, during my junior and senior years, I became a mom when my younger sisters came to live with me.

I did travel some every year and my first adventure was a trip to Fayetteville, Arkansas. This is where Chi Omega was founded, and my freshman year was its 100th anniversary. Several of us decided to head down there for the celebration. What was funny was that the women I traveled with weren't friends of mine or even girls I hung out with but that was part of the fun. You get to know people when you are in a car with them for hours! For example, I never will forget how much Natalie and Tracey LOVED the soundtrack to The Lion King (yes, another reminder of how old I am).

Another eye opener for that trip was this: the first night, there are probably over 1,0000 women running around, most of them blond, with big boobs and rich looking — basically, my arch nemesis. The president of Chi Omega stood up and addressed us, "Ladies, take a look to your right, and now to your left. These are your sisters!" I was floored. These were the women that seconds ago, I had been judging. Now, I realized that they were my sisters! These women and I had a bond, Chi Omega, and we would help each other. I could go anywhere around the US and find refuge in a Chi Omega house. That was really eye-opening for me and it always stuck with me.

The summer after my freshman year was my second trip on a plane. I had itchy feet and now at 18 I had become "Target #1". I was locked and loaded with a credit card which I didn't really understand but was fully able to use stupidly. I went to Las Vegas, where one of my best friends from high school was living. It was certainly another "eye-opening" experience but different than you would imagine since I was too young to gamble. What I remembered the most from that experience was when we would drive by the "ghetto" of Las Vegas, and I would be thinking... "Really? That's the Ritz Carlton compared to where I grew up."

5

～

Thug Life

I didn't go anywhere substantial after my sophomore year. By then I had entered my major studies, Ceramic Engineering, and was researching "Piezoelectrics" which means mechanical electronics. The materials were supplied by Motorola (which was the beginning of my love for them) but the research was being done for the Department of Defense and Allied Signal in Kansas City. I did such a great job during the school year that I ended up with a summer internship at Allied Signal (which was later bought by Honeywell.) I had to have "Government Clearance" which was a little stressful due to my "Youthful Stealing Sprees" but luckily those records really were sealed!

I loved working there – the people were amazing and I learned so much from them. I worked with an old Jewish guy who always said to me... "We need to put some meat on them bones," and then would feed me! He was the King of purchasing! If you wanted a couch for your office, he would call it "A horizontal something or other" that sounded so complicated and important, that no one would turn him down. His lab was awesome, fully stocked, and comfortable. I worked with Bob Presley who told everyone he was related to Elvis and Charlie who would walk outside to smoke and complain about not being able to smoke inside anymore. They were a great team!!

This was the summer of 1996.

I was living with my pregnant best friend Marline, her husband (or soon-to-be) Richard, and daughter Tylor (TT) in KCMO. Basically, I slept on the couch. We lived on 35th and Brooklyn. Brooklyn is located between Prospect and Troost. For all my old-school peeps, you might remember an HBO movie that came out about that time called 27th and Prospect. Needless to say, I was pretty much in the middle of gang territory. Kind of... Our neighbors knew me and would take care of me but this summer I was taking public transportation.

Here was my route:

In the morning I would catch the bus at 35th and Brooklyn and ride it to 39th and Brooklyn. I would then catch a bus on 39th St and Brooklyn to 39th and Troost. There I would take the bus to 85th and Troost. It was the afternoon when it got a little more interesting. As I mentioned, Brooklyn is in between Troost and Prospect. That summer I would wake up to news reports of shootings within a mile of where I was waiting for the bus. I was "protected" in my neighborhood, but I wasn't in my hood all of the time. While waiting for the bus, cars would slow down and say shit to me, throw stuff at me, etc... so one day while waiting for the bus, I passed a note to a little girl who was always riding her bike on that street. It said, "My name is Daisie, I live at blah blah blah, and if you see someone grab me, call blah blah blah."

This was before the days of cell phones. I had to make sure someone would notice if I disappeared. Luckily, nothing ever happened to me, but I ain't gonna lie, I was nervous at times.

6

∽

First Love

The summer after my junior year I took a trip to Florida and the Bahamas with my boyfriend as a graduation present for him. It was during this trip that I learned that before I agree to marry anyone I would first travel with them. My boyfriend at the time, E, would not listen to anything I said when it came to directions. We would argue and argue...until of course I was proven right and then he would be even more pissed off.

We spent the first couple of days in the Ft. Lauderdale/Miami area where we hung out at the beach or pool and my pale, pasty ass was always applying sunblock. I would say in my sexy voice, "Baby you want me to put sunblock on your back." His reply would be, "Baby, black people don't burn". So, as you can imagine on day three, E is complaining that he is in pain. He was so sunburnt that he was blistering!! I hated being right that time.

The next part of our trip was to the Bahamas. It was supposed to be a cruise until they found out I was only 20 so instead we spent the day on one of the islands, exploring and snorkeling. Back then you didn't need a passport to visit the Bahamas, only a birth certificate, so no passport stamps for either one of us, too.

We stayed in a beautiful hotel and went snorkeling. To make E feel better, even with all the sunblock I added, I still ended up with a bad sunburn on my ass from snorkeling and it hurt to sit for days. Oh, and to make the journey even more eventful...on the way back from the Bahamas I lost my luggage and had to buy more clothes. Someone had taken my suitcase instead of theirs. We were headed to meet Mickey Mouse in Orlando and I couldn't show up in my bikini!! Not a poor college student's greatest dream, but I made it work and we probably had the best time of the whole trip there! I did eventually get my luggage back, but for some reason all of my underwear was missing and of course all of the cool souvenirs I had purchased before this point. The bastards!

E moved to Iowa to start his career and we had our moments during my senior year. At one point he even asked me to drop out of school, marry him and move to bum fuck Iowa. Wait one sec...UH... HELL to the NO!! Really? Maybe if I was a freshman, but I only had one year to go, and I wasn't dropping out of school to be someone's housewife in the middle of nowhere Iowa.

7

~

Senior... What is Taking So Friggin Long... Year

As I mentioned I went to an engineering school in a very small town. The most exciting thing to do there was to go to Applebee's and it didn't open until I was a SENIOR! The second thing to do was go to the Super Walmart and I worked there...so it wasn't that much fun for me.

I didn't drink in college (remember the part about my mom being a drug addict and alcoholic) so I didn't drink at frat parties, and I really didn't even go to them. Occasionally I would go with one of my sorority sisters and would always get a warm welcome... "Oh You're Daisie!!! Let me go get your Dr Pepper" (Yes, I was absolutely addicted to Dr. Pepper in college). It was always fun to hear, "Oh you're Daisie". I had always hated my name growing up because of all the nicknames; Daisy Dukes, Daisy Fuentes, Lazy Daisy, Crazy Daisy, etc... but in college I realized I was a brand. There were very few Daisies in the world, especially in the "Engineering" world. I decided to OWN being Daisie. I mean come on...how many Daisies do you know?

During my senior year, I was taking care of my eleven-year-old sister, trying to graduate, and trying to get a job, all at the same time. The way it worked back then was that you would fly out for Interview "Windows" where they would invite hundreds of seniors from all over the US, wine and dine them, and try to entice you to join their company. I only had two companies on my radar, and both were in the Phoenix area. Motorola and Intel.

I stalked them both for a year. If they were anywhere within 100 miles I would drive to them to give them my resume and expose them to the "Daisieness". In July 1997 after my trip with E, I was in a car accident and totaled my car. I had planned on driving to St. Louis the following weekend to present my resume to Motorola at a job fair. Luckily a good friend of mine, Shahid, drove me. I talked to a woman named Melissa, who was awesome by the way, and she said that the career fair was for experienced people but Motorola did have a University department and she would pass my resume on. From then on, I emailed, faxed, mailed, and called every person I could find contact information for. I sent Melissa Thanksgiving, Christmas, and other cards.

On Valentine's Day, 1998 Melissa called me and invited me to the Interview Window in AZ, in March. Well DUH!! I jumped at it. (Forgetting of course that I had planned my first REAL spring break trip to New York City to visit my friend Shahid who was getting his PhD at Rutgers.) No worries, Motorola flew me from NYC to AZ and I got to do both!

In the meantime, Motorola-Austin was visiting our campus for the first time in years. I didn't get automatically selected for an interview because I didn't have the right degree or GPA but the trick back then was to attend their "informational sessions" and talk your way into an interview. So I sat, practically bouncing in my chair for the session to be over so I could WOW them. After the presentation, I walked confidently over to the presenter and said, "Hi, I'm Daisie Hobson," and you know what he said? "Oh, You're Daisie! I have a whole file on you and we want to set up an interview with you."

After shipping my sister to live with her dad, I went to both windows and I had thought that the days of being "Mama Daisie" were over.

8

∿

A Spring Break I Will Never Forget!!

Besides securing a job two months before I even graduated, the real adventure of my senior year was Spring Break! I know I kind of glazed over it in the previous chapter, but it was actually pretty substantial in ways I wouldn't know until much later. Shahid had been an MS student at UMR when I was an undergrad. We would run into each other in the lab late at night. I was doing research for one professor, and he was doing research for another. He was the teacher's assistant (TA) my junior year, a job I took over and LOVED my senior year. We struck up conversations and a friendship over ceramic powders etc... The thing with ceramics or semiconductors, there is a lot of waiting!

He was worldly in my eyes. He was a Muslim from Pakistan who had got his BS from Rutgers and was now living in the middle of MO. We had great conversations about all kinds of things, including music, which led him to invite me to St. Louis for a classical music concert. We had a marvelous dinner, where there were no prices on the menu, he shopped for cashmere sweaters that cost more than my rent, and we listened to great music, oh and I didn't embarrass him. He was so thoughtful that the next concert we went to was Winton Marsalis because I mentioned

I loved jazz. We were great friends, but it didn't go from there mostly because I was in an on and off again relationship with E.

He left for Rutgers as I started my senior year, but he invited me to visit him. Well DUH!!! Oh, of course, I would. I had always wanted to go to New York! So, I booked a trip for my Spring Break, which unfortunately didn't correspond with his Spring Break and he ended up being crazy busy so I ended up spending time with his dad (who was exiled from Pakistan), his friends, and his girlfriend...who by the way looked a lot like me. I guess if he couldn't get the real thing, he had to go with second best. Hey...I'm just saying...

Even though he was busy, he did spend one day taking me to NYC and showing me around a bit. One of the attractions he took me to was the World Trade Center – the Twin Towers. We went to the 106th Floor – The Windows of the World restaurant and had a glass of wine. Unfortunately, it was a cloudy day so all we saw were clouds but just the trip up in the elevator was something I had never experienced. I think the highest I had ever gone before was in the 40s, so 106 floors up and superfast, was amazing! I have always loved heights, so I wasn't afraid, more like in awe. Three years later, a plane would crash into the building and change the world forever. I am lucky that I got to be a part of history in experiencing The Windows of the World.

Another fun part of the trip was going clubbin'! Shahid couldn't go, but as I mentioned I loved to dance so a couple of his friends and I went out. As you can imagine, the club scene in NYC is every night, all night long! It was nothing like I had ever experienced in KC, and truth be told, I was afraid of drug addicts running after me with needles but once I got there and was part of the scene, I realized how ridiculous that was.

We went to one of P Diddy's (Puff Daddy or Sean Combs or whatever his name was back then) clubs. He made a brief entrance but I didn't care. I was dancing! Shahid's friends were more wallflower-type guys, so they let me do my thing without cock blocking. I ended up seeing this super sexy guy and I decided to approach him (I never said I was shy, timid, or bashful). As I approached him though, he started smoking. I went up to him and said, "You are too fine to be smoking." He smashed the cigarette out and we spent the rest of the night talking. He was Haitian, so he spoke with a super sexy French accent that had me swooning... So, he was another collectible.

We became pen pals, he joined the army, I moved to AZ, he visited me in AZ, I visited him in Seattle, WA and that was it.... Another tale to be told in a less PG-rated book.

Shahid and I parted as friends. We catch up every five years or so which means we are past due.

9

∽

New Grads!

I graduated from college in May 1998 and back then they were throwing money at engineers. Many of my friends had multiple offers from great companies. I personally only wanted to work for Motorola (Intel was my second choice) and although I didn't have the degree or the GPA they wanted I ended up with job offers from both Motorola Phoenix and Motorola Austin. I decided on Phoenix because it looked different than Missouri. Texas looked just like Missouri but HOT. I figured if I was going to be hot I wanted to be in a place that didn't look like where I came from.

I ended up accepting the job offer in March but since I didn't have any money I didn't take any time off after graduation. My mom and I drove cross country from Missouri to Arizona to start my new life. I was so broke at this point that I had to take a signature loan to pay for the trip and living expenses for a couple of weeks. It was stressful, to say the least. So here I was this little white girl in a strange city, surrounded by a lot of people who looked like me, and people who didn't look like me and spoke Spanish and I was middle class. If I thought college was shocking being middle class was even more so.

What was great about this move though was that there had to be hundreds of new grads who invaded Phoenix, Tempe, Mesa, and Scottsdale that year. Between Motorola, Boeing, Honeywell, and Intel there were young people with money all over the place. Men would come up to me and my girlfriends and say, "I make blah blah blah" and we would laugh and say, "We make more than that". That summer we partied harder than I ever did in college, and I still didn't drink. We would start going out on Wednesday and only rest on Tuesday nights before we started again. We were young, had no real responsibilities, and had money to burn.

We would travel in the blink of an eye. We would get emails on Tuesday about cheap flights to wherever that weekend and we would go. Since we came from all over the country, we had friends or family we could stay with and did so because even though we had money to burn we were still cheap. At least once a month we were somewhere: Chicago, Seattle, New York, Las Vegas, San Diego, Los Angeles, and Austin to name only a few.

10

∽

Federales

Of course, since we were so close to Mexico, we would take road trips to Rocky Point (Puerto Penesco). Now remember the part where I mentioned we were cheap? Well, sometimes we would rent a house and throw like 20 people in the house. Other times, though, we couldn't get a house and would get hotel rooms and share it with like 6 people. Not a good idea at the time. The Federales with their rifles would watch to see who went in and out of each room and if they counted too many people they would harass you. A few of the guys ended up sleeping in the van and let Sumi and I sleep in real beds. Not that they noticed they were so wasted!

So, my road trip to Mexico was my "third" International experience and this time it felt different, even though I didn't get a stamp in my passport. Besides the language difference, most merchants spoke English, but there were very obvious differences. Like bartering for example, in the US, if it says it's a $1.00 you pay $1.00. In Mexico, I found that you could "negotiate." I learned to carry a lot of five-dollar bills around and offer to pay 5 dollars for everything. (I have a large family remember? And at this time I was still trying to find everyone's "unique" gifts from wherever I went.) I also found that trying to convert money in my head was hard. When we had to pay in Mexican pesos we usually gave them way too much money, but it didn't matter; we figured they needed it more than we did.

A major difference that I found the most irritating was the corruption. Every time we were leaving Rocky Point we would get pulled over and a police officer would ask us for money. The trick was on them though because we always had a Spanish speaker with us who would negotiate the bribe down. It sucked though because by the time we were leaving, I was pretty much broke. It was like... "Really dude!! I spent all my money with your people!" We were lucky, though, I heard of horror stories where people would be forced to go to the ATM and withdraw money and a very rare case where they would be thrown in jail. A few $20 bills here and there, were nothing compared to those experiences.

Regardless, it was a learning experience. I learned a few Spanish words to be respectful and to help me negotiate. I went to my first strip club, I hitch-hiked for the first time (only to go three blocks), I celebrated the 4th of July in a country that couldn't care less, and I attempted to blow up a car. Well, not me exactly but the crazy guys I went down there with. Oh, and it was an abandoned shelled-out car that I am sure other people tried to blow up before. At this point though, where we went in Rocky Point didn't look too much different than Arizona. The desert was the same, the few houses we saw were the same stucco design and the people were the same. It wasn't as "different" as I thought it would be.

Those were the good ol' days. That first year in Arizona was awesome! We had a blast traveling, partying, making new friends, and just being young, dumb, and free! As our leases ran out on our apartments though many of us started buying houses, getting into serious relationships, getting more responsibility at work and in general - growing up. I bought my first house when I was 22 and my family moved in a few months later.

I had a few more hurrahs to live through before I became a mom again.

11

⌒

Finally! A Stamp in My Passport

I didn't move into an apartment when I moved to Arizona. Remember that awesome recruiter I mentioned, Melissa? Well as luck would have it, she had just bought a house and wanted a roommate since she traveled so much. I lived with her for about six months before she moved back to San Diego. Then I moved in with two guys I worked with. Al had just bought a house and needed roommates, so Willie D. and I moved in. I was the only girl and I refused to share a bathroom with them, so I got the master bedroom. The three of us were good friends and we traveled often together.

Al was Columbian from New Jersey and Willie D was Puerto Rican from Philly. They certainly brought a lot of culture and color into our little home. Willie D and I were blessed that Al loved to cook but unfortunately, neither liked to clean or do dishes...LOL! We got along great and respected each other.

At the house, we had a stream of visitors, and one was Ricky. He was from the Bahamas originally and had gone to Tuskegee. I was in awe of him. He was a gentleman through and through and could cook a mean jerk chicken among other things. Due to some hiccup with immigration, he had to go back to the Bahamas to get it worked out. He invited all of us to visit him, but I was the only one who was able to go. I was looking forward to going and finally getting a stamp on my passport. A couple of months previously, I had driven from Cincinnati, OH with my college roommate JL to Windsor, Canada, and didn't get my passport stamped. I was getting upset...PLEASE WON'T SOMEONE STAMP MY PASSPORT?

I flew into Fort Lauderdale and then took a boat across. I am sure you are asking...the same boat you took in college? Funny you should ask but yes. And yes, the same thing happened. To avoid having my luggage stolen this time, I decorated it a little and I put all my underwear on top (so they would know it was a girl's bag.) Well, when I got off the boat my bag was there but...Some bastard stole all my underwear!! Seriously!! Really?? Underwear? Gross! I figured they just went through the bags and swiped everything that was on top. In my case they got underwear.

I had brought Ricky a bunch of mail, so when we arrived at his house, I opened my suitcase to get his mail and realized that all my underwear (and a few super cute dresses) were gone. How do you tell a man (who is not your boyfriend) and his family that you need to go shopping for underwear? Embarrassingly, that's how. To make it worse, Ricky's mom had a joke underwear drawer. It was the family joke, to give their mom super sexy underwear. She was like "Baby, you can have anything in this drawer" as she pulled out sexy thongs and crotchless panties. I was about to die because of course she did this in front of Ricky and his brothers. JUST KILL ME NOW!

I was right to ask for death at that point, the next day Ricky takes me to a "boutique" to go underwear shopping because of course there is no Walmart on the island. Of course, the super cute women in the "boutique" thought we were "together" and were showing him super sexy underwear for me. What I wouldn't have done for some granny panties at that point.

I escaped that experience with as much dignity as I could manage and just tried to enjoy my time with him and his family. His family's house was magnificent. We picked mangos and avocados from the tree in the backyard and just ate them. I ate my first turtle soup (yes with a real turtle shell in the pot). I fell in love with everything conch and Bahamian.

The people were amazing, so friendly and welcoming. There were tons of mixed-race couples and most people seemed genuinely happy. I didn't want to leave!!

Almost all of his family was either in construction or tourism, so we got the hook-up for everything! We got to do everything I had wanted to do with E but for free. It wasn't that though, it was being on the other side of tourism, going where the locals go, and being a part of the community that made it an amazing experience.

I was lucky with this experience and now whenever I travel I try making friends with the locals and find out where they go to party. I guarantee it's more fun and cheaper!

12

⌇

Traveling for Work Take 1

When I joined Motorola, I joined it as a Manufacturing Engineering Rotation Program (MERP) Engineer. We were to change positions and manufacturing sites every four months for a year. This was an amazing experience. Not only would we get to learn different parts of the semiconductor manufacturing process, but we would get to work in different fabs (semi-conductor fabrication plants are called "fabs") around the US and Internationally! Originally I was scheduled for two sites in Arizona and my last would be in Malaysia. I was so excited I got my passport within two weeks of the announcement. I was so ready to go to Malaysia! This was part of the reason I wanted to work for Motorola. They had fabs all over the world and I wanted to visit them all!

Then the US embassy in Tunisia was bombed and all international rotations were canceled. I was bummed but I was excited about going to Austin to do a rotation there. Then that was canceled as well. Again, I was bummed that I wasn't able to travel but I figured it was only a matter of time, so I chose to do two rotations in 8" fabs (the largest at the time) and one in backend manufacturing (which is what they did in Malaysia). I learned a lot from these experiences and met some great people who are still my friends today.

When the year was over, I went back to my original fab which was going through some pretty dynamic changes, and in less than three months I was transferred to a GaAs fab. GaAs, for you curious cats...stands for Gallium Arsenide. If you aren't a nerd like me you can skip this next paragraph...

Most semiconductors start with Si (Silicon) substrates which are made from sand and are a part of nature. You add Oxygen and other metals, circuits, transistors, and other fun stuff and you get a microchip. Well, GaAs wafers are not natural, are harder to make, and are more fragile. When the largest Si wafer was 8", they were just transitioning to 6" in GaAs. The process of making GaAs wafers is more complex which also makes them more expensive. By the time some of these wafers make it to the end of the line, they are worth millions!

While working at the GaAs fab I had three positions. They loved me and I was asked to lead a team to investigate the cause of wafer breakage. I found the cause in a third of the time they allocated. I saved them millions of dollars in losses, and I got tons of awards but I was miserable! Before I was on this team I kept telling people I felt like an over-paid monkey. I would get all dressed up in my clean room (monkey) suit, go to my machine, press a button, wait, write a number down, press a button, wait, write a number down...rinse and repeat. I would go for hours without talking to anyone, white noise gave me headaches and my back hurt from standing for hours. Really? Have you met me? Luckily, I was put on the wafer breakage team where I actually got to *talk* to people, which is what most engineers hate to do, and which is why I think I finished the project faster than they expected.

After that experience, I asked to be transferred to another division, one that had more people interfacing. I ended up in Factory Planning and my two fabs were 6" fabs in Mesa and Scotland! I knew for sure that I would be visiting Scotland very shortly. Yeah, not so much...

13

~

Vegas Baby!

Since we had a fab in Scotland we had a few Scottish people in Arizona and my itchy feet always led me to them to talk about where they came from, cultural things, etc... What was funny about all the Scottish people though was that they would all say the same thing. "If you ever go to Scotland, let me know and I will tell you what pub to go to." Really? Is there anything else to do in Scotland besides going to the pub? I would later read books based in Scotland...and the answer was very clear...No.

Working with the Scottish also taught me that there were differences in English. Sometimes I would listen to them and afterward be like...Was he speaking English? In Spanish we say "Despacio por favor"...speak slowly, please. I wish I would have known how to say that in Scottish English. They used funny terms like boot instead of trunk, but the funniest difference happened during a rainstorm in Scotland. We had conference calls with them once a week in the morning (their afternoon). One day we heard all kinds of noise on their side, so we asked what was going on. She says, well we are in a "porta cabin" and it's raining. All we hear on our side though is "porta cabin" and I know in my mind I was thinking, "porta potties"? A few of us laugh and say, "What?" Then she explains that they are in temporary housing, porta cabins, due to construction. We finally get that she means "trailers".

Funny but I digress...

Living in the Phoenix area meant that Vegas was easily accessible. I had been there several times, both driving and flying. I even took my brother Sean there for his 21st birthday. There was one time though that was most memorable. Once upon a time, you could fly to Vegas from Phoenix for $60 round trip. It was awesome! A group of us would fly there after work on Friday, stay up all night gambling and whatever, and then fly home around 10 in the morning on Saturday.

When I say group, I mostly mean the people I worked with. It included my boss, the guy I dated in another department, and other people in our group. My boyfriend and I were still a secret, so we were keeping things low-key. For the most part, it was a bunch of "singles" who wanted to kick it in Vegas. Well, the most memorable trip was the third and last trip of its kind or at least the last that I participated in.

It started as normal as usual but as we were waiting for the flight my throat started itching, so I asked for tea instead of booze on the flight. Not that I drank at this time but still... By the time we got to Vegas and took the limo to our regular casino, I could tell I was coming down with a cold. Me being Daisie though, I soldiered through it. I gambled, ate, and drank, hell I don't even remember most of what we did though since I was walking around in a fog.

We mostly played Blackjack. I always came home with either the same amount of money I left with or more so I considered myself a winner, but my boss was riskier than I was. He made very risky bets and was very lucky. So lucky that most of the time we went we were comp'd a room. We usually didn't use it but in this case, I was so sick I couldn't hang so I asked to use the room. We go get the room and I attempt to pass out. Next thing I know, the door opens, and my boss and another coworker enter. I wasn't asleep so I could hear everything. I thought she would just head to the bed, and he would leave. So much for that...

The next thing I hear is kissing, then shuffling... and then I leave. Oh, and did I forget to mention that my boss was engaged? I am sick as a dog, and you are making out in the other bed? And you didn't even wait long enough for me to fall asleep? WTF!!!

Needless to say, I was not happy, and our relationship was never the same. Luckily I got worse and since this was the weekend before Thanksgiving I ended up taking Monday, Tuesday, and Wednesday off along with the holiday. He sent me an email. I still can't believe he documented that shit! He apologized etc... but I tried to just ignore it. It wasn't my business, I wasn't mad that he was cheating, I was mad because I didn't get any sleep. I was also disappointed in men in general.

I didn't have time to harp on it too much. Many people blame the 2001 recession on 9-11 but those of us in electronics, specifically semiconductors, know that the recession started at the end of 2000 and in Taiwan. Taiwan was putting a limit/ban/higher tax on imports, which included wafers. Taiwan at the time was one of the main areas of back-end manufacturing (meaning they took finished wafers, cut them into the finished die, and then packaged them). Oh, and did I mention a huge earthquake in Taiwan where Motorola and several other chip companies lost billions of dollars in wafers? Yes, this happened in November 2000 and as a planner, I had to change my demand in my front-end manufacturing, which I did. Only to discover that Taiwan didn't want our business and in February 2001 the layoffs began. The episode with my boss was a distant memory.

14

~

Anger, Resentment, 12 Steps, and Other Such Pleasantries

I didn't get laid off, but I did leave Motorola not too long afterward and went to another company where I was subsequently laid off three months later. In the meantime, my family had moved in with me and now I was responsible for more than just me.

In August 1999, just before my 22nd birthday, I bought a three-bedroom, 2 ½ bath townhouse. I was proud of myself, and I felt like an adult. A few months later my mom's rental house had some issues (including ½ of the house falling in) so I invited them to come live with me. Truth be told that was part of the reason I bought such a big place. My entire life has been about helping them and this felt like it was meant to be. My sisters, Maisie and Mary Jane, my youngest brother Stevie, and mom moved in with me. Sean and Jimmy stayed in KS. It was crowded but it was home.

When I was laid off I was devastated because no one had ever said "No" to me. I never failed at anything! I may have not always been the smartest, but everyone loved me, and I worked hard. This wasn't the only blow I got that year, Maisie ran away, I broke up with the man I thought I was going to marry, my mom was going to a bar every night instead of coming home and my schizophrenic brother also moved in with us. Piece of cake, right? Not so much but I dealt with it. I got a part-time job at the mall selling jeans and a full-time job filing. I did what I needed to do to pay my bills like my mom had always done. I didn't look at the jobs as "beneath me" - I looked at it as a "means to an end."

I ended up getting a job at a medical device company that shall not be named because it ended badly for all parties. I didn't show my true "Daisieness" at the time of the interview and was hired but they wanted me to be a robot, or a clone and this Daisie is neither. The job turned into a nightmare and even though I was finding comfort and clarity in Adult Children for Alcoholics meetings, as a big sister for the Big Sister Big Brother program, and as a core member for Life Teen, I was very unhappy. I was miserable at work and bitter at home. I had nothing besides reading that made me happy and I wasn't doing much of that.

Except for my third-grade year, I have always been "Daisie" and when you have a name like mine, it's almost like people expect you to be happy-go-lucky, innocent, and full of fun. By the time I left Motorola, I had worked there for 3 and a half years and had seven positions. People would especially ask for me, not because I was a "brilliant" engineer but because I was "enthusiastic." I wanted to get a business card made that said: Daisie Hobson, Enthusiastic Engineer. The new EE!

Of course, I was an expert at wearing masks. I had been wearing masks since I was a child and had to go to school with bruises and keep teachers and parents from asking too many questions. I wasn't happy at work, but I did what I had to do and looked for something to "Make Me Happy."

One weekend, I took my little sister to West Wind Flying School in Phoenix. She got to go up in a small plane and fly the plane. The owner of West Wind was a Big Brother in the Big Brother Big Sister (BBBS) program and every year he took the "littles" up. I was so jealous! If she had gone up in a 172 Cessna instead of a 152 I would have been able to go. But no, they went up, and while I was waiting I went to the front desk to ask for more information. I asked how much the program cost and they said about $8,000 to $10,000 I frowned and started to leave. As

I turned around to leave the lady at the front desk said six magic words, "Student loans will pay for it." DONE!

Ever since I saw the movie Iron Eagle, I knew I wanted to be a pilot. Hell, my long-term plans were to be an astronaut, which is why I went into engineering. Unfortunately, a collision with a Lincoln when I was 15 ruined those plans but I still longed to be a pilot. I had nothing in my life that I "loved." I looked at my life and had many regrets so I thought to myself "I don't want to turn 50 and say 'I wish I would have learned how to fly.'"

The summer after being laid off, and just before 9-11, I started the process of joining the Air Force, hoping to test high enough to be a pilot. The Friday after 9-11, I was taking the test to qualify for Officer Training School in downtown Phoenix and during the next to last section a bomb threat made my test null and void. It answered my prayers or whether or not I should join the military during war time. In October, I joined the medical device company and six months later I was on my way to get my private pilot's license, twelve months later... I was laid off - again.

15

~

Masks

As I look back on it now, the friends I mentioned in Chapter 1 probably never even knew what was going on in my house (or in my head). I learned to wear masks. As an adult working with teens in a church program, I often talk about masks and why we wear them. I think over time I wore more and more masks. I had a different mask for every environment. One for work, one for church, one for home, one for my boyfriend, and one for friends. Makes me wonder if anyone ever really knew the real me.

I want to say that I only had one mask when I was younger but thinking about it in more depth, I probably had at least three. One for home, the protector of my brothers and sisters, the bitch that stood up to my father but then still a child that runs and hides in my room to study and escape. Another for school is the happy-go-lucky girl named Daisie who is always bubbly, smiley, and always in a good mood. Lastly for my friends and their family, a little more vulnerable than I want to be but still strong because I don't want to seem weak in front of others.

There are lots of studies and articles and stories about "African Americans" who "assimilate" into "white" society but really? Don't we all? Even as a very obviously white woman/girl, I had to assimilate in order to fit in. I had to assimilate into every situation I was in, whether it was a white girl in a racially diverse environment or a poor girl in a "rich" environment. I don't think people realize how often we actually have to adapt to our surroundings. Even when I became an engineer I had to assimilate into the "male" world.

Assimilation and wearing masks are two different worlds though. Wearing a mask means that you are hiding from the world, the "who you are on the inside" isn't the "who you are" that you show to the world. You don't want anyone to see the real you. If you took off that mask and looked inside of it you would see your fears, your insecurities, and sometimes your truths.

Assimilation means that you accept the world that you live in, and you try to live in that world. It's not your dream or your fantasy world, but you accept it as reality and you make it happen.

In my case, at least as a pre-teen, I was wearing a mask to hide my pain. My stepfather was a true con artist. Everyone, except for the people who lived with him, loved him. He could sell ice to Eskimos. I always wondered why no one helped us. My mother was the youngest of five kids, why didn't they help us? If one of my sisters and her kids went through what my mom went through... OH HELL NO!! That's where the ghetto Craisiedaze comes out.

16

～

Dreaming of a Rescue

I used to dream of being rescued. Someone who would make the pain go away. No one ever did. My mother finally rescued us by leaving him. We went through years of abuse. I was a light sleeper as a child. I would wake up to my mom crying and bleeding. I would beg her to leave him, but she couldn't/wouldn't...whatever the excuse was. I never knew what triggered those attacks. I would wake up to my mom crying because she was in a car accident because she was drinking and driving, she was self-medicating to come home, or because he beat her.

The time that stands out the most was when I went into the living room and blood was running down my beautiful mother's face. I think I was about eight years old. I had heard them fighting in the back patio and I heard him hit her. She went down hard and hit her head on the concrete. He left but my mom didn't. She promised she would leave him and protect us, but she didn't. At least once a year we would call the police, but he always talked his way out of it. As I got older I got more obstinate, I tried to protect my mom and my brothers and sisters but nothing I ever did made a difference.

I found out at the age of nine that he wasn't my father and I celebrated!! His blood wasn't mine! I didn't have that hatred and ugliness running through my veins. I remember about that time saying to him in a very manner of fact, adult-like manner, "It's not the physical abuse, it's the mental abuse". Seriously, I was a made-for-TV movie, an adult in a pre-teen body. It wasn't just about him hitting us, it was his mental abuse. I felt like less than nothing. If I hadn't been as good in school as I was, I would probably be a statistic today. If I had listened to his propaganda, I would be a racist mother with ten kids on welfare, blaming the government for my choices.

He abused me from my earliest memories until I was thirteen years old. My brother Sean and I tried our best to protect the younger kids from the abuse, but one memory comes to mind. Jimmy, who was probably six or seven had taken some money from the change can to buy some candy, and "the Monster" found out about it. He didn't spank Jimmy with his hands, or even a "switch". He hit Jimmy with a board, 22 times. That event broke my heart on so many different levels. It taught me that I didn't have any power and that I couldn't protect them. It showed me what real evil was and it taught me shame. Shame that I didn't take those lashings for him, shame that I didn't stop him from taking the money, shame that I lived.

The summer before I turned 13, the Monster got pissed at me or them for some reason or another, and I being the bitch that he always called me to be, stood up to him. Normally he only "hit" my mother. Her scars are not from his fists but from hitting something on the way down, like a concrete step or a stove. (YES, I remember every scar almost as clearly as she does). As for us, it was more like crazy spankings and mental abuse, but now I was a young woman and I looked exactly like my mother.

I don't know if that was what tipped him over the edge, but we started screaming at each other and the next thing I know he sucker-punched me and I ended up landing in a bunch of unpacked boxes (we had just moved). I remember waking up seconds later and running away screaming, he grabbed me by my throat and squeezed until I passed out again. He left me there in the kitchen. I woke up, checked on the kids, and went to my room. I went to school the next day with his fingerprints on my neck, the school called the police, and he sweet-talked his way out of it.

A few weeks later my mom finally left him, and we moved to

Lawrence, Kansas to live with her brother, my uncle Jim. I hated leaving my school and my friends, but I was glad to leave the monster. Many months later I asked my mom, "Why after eleven years and many scars, did you finally decide to leave him?" You know what she said? "He wouldn't get a job."

They had five kids and his cons and selling drugs weren't helping. My mom begged him to get a job and his response was... "What do you want me to do - pump gas?" she said, "Yes, pump gas! I am just a waitress". He replied, "You are the best fucking waitress in the world!" My mom said, "Well you can be the best fucking gas man in the world! I need help!" He still refused to get a real job, so she left him.

We were some of the lucky ones. In college, when I finally realized that I needed help, I attended group sessions with other students who were still, to that day, as adults, being abused. Sometimes it was physical but in a lot of cases, it was mental, which can be worse.

The Monster used to go around and tell people that he fell in love with me first and my mother second. He was a predator, and I have no tolerance for abuse. I may wear a lot of masks, and I may smile in your face and pretend to like you because my name is Daisie, and I love everyone, but if you fuck with me, my family, or anyone I care about... that is when you really see that you can "Take me out of the ghetto, but you can't take the ghetto out of me!" (Original title of this book).

Years later I was still trying to figure out the real me, trying to figure out who Daisie really was. I tried taking flying lessons, I tried being a Big Sister, I tried getting involved with the church and I even tried the 12 Steps. No one ever really got me, even in America I felt like a stranger in a strange land, maybe that is why I like being different in foreign countries.

17

∽

Exorcising Mom

My time at the medical device company taught me that I wasn't a robot or a clone and that I needed interaction with people! From there I went into sales because it seemed like the natural progression. I first joined a health insurance company. It was a Christian-based company and seemed to have the same ideals as me. The problem was - it was 100% commission. Everyone in the office except for me was married and if they didn't make sales - the bills still got paid. In my case...not so much...

My mom and at least three siblings were living with me. Mom had gotten laid off too so if I didn't produce, the bills didn't get paid! I wasn't a bad salesperson, but I had my bad weeks. It got worse when I found out that most of my clients were getting denied. I would promise them coverage and then due to the stupid MIB – Medical Information Board, they would be denied. They would call me crying and I didn't handle it too well. I would feel their pain and it would affect my performance.

About a year after health insurance sales and other mind-numbing positions (including working for a call center) I moved into a technical sales position. I was making a salary plus commission, and it seemed to be a good fit for me. It was in telecom and half of the salespeople didn't understand the technology, but I did. I could sell you a T1 that made your current internet look like hamsters were powering it and I was doing fairly well personally.

I was ministering to about 30 teens on a weekly basis, and I had started a weekly teen AA meeting. I thought I was getting all the "love and support" I needed but I don't think I was. My mom was still going to the bar before she came home, and I was home being "mom" by cooking and helping with the homework.

I bet you are thinking...you need counseling! Well, I was in a lot of counseling. At one point, I was seeing regular counselors, a nun, and a Irish priest. It was the Irish priest that may or may not have changed my mother's life. Depending on what you believe.

One night, at a session, I described my life which included cooking, cleaning, and homework help. How I felt obligated to do it since my mom was at the bar, and how I "had to save" my family. He proposes something I would have never imagined outside of a movie. He said I needed to exorcise that demon out of my mother. He gives me a medal with salt on it, a bag of salt, some holy water, and a prayer. He said, when your mom is sleeping one night, sprinkle this salt and holy water around her bed and say, "Devil be gone!" and I am sure some other stuff that I have forgotten.

At this point, I am willing to try anything, so I do it! I wear the holy medal; I sprinkle the salt and holy water and I say the words and then I forget about it. A few weeks later, we are all hanging out on the porch and my mom says. "The bar is closing". The bar my mom went to was across the street from where we lived. Arizona is a no-tolerance state so any amount of alcohol will get you a DUI so I told her that she couldn't drink and drive, which is why she found a bar across the street. She would drink, walk home and my brother would go get the car.

When the bar closed mom would come home every night and drink at home. She still drank but at least she drank at home where her kids could find her, where she was safe, and where she could help with the little things like cooking and homework. I don't really know if I "exorcised" my mom and a demon, but I was glad she was home, and I wasn't responsible for her kids...AGAIN!

18

~

San Fran Cisco

Even with what little money I was making and the family I was now supporting, I still managed to travel. I went to NYC with a friend I met while we were waiting for the post-911 bomb threat. We were both taking the Officer Training School (OTS) test to become officers in the Air Force when the bomb threat came. It was the Friday after 9-11-2001 and although we both wanted to join we felt like this was a sign from God.

We had to leave all of our stuff there, so we headed to a local restaurant and spent the next couple of hours telling our stories while waiting for the signal to come back. We were the only women in the test, and we became friends. A year, almost to the date, later we traveled to NYC to pay respects to the dead. I remember driving down one street and feeling the dread and melancholy. It was a street from the news, a street that had ash and smoke blowing down it, it was the street that was changed forever and even a year later we felt it. This was a hard trip for me, and I felt the loss and pain.

Over the next couple of years, I think I traveled to a few weddings and other random events...including an emergency trip to Florida where JL saved me from a serious depression. Back then, I went to at least two to three weddings a year. My sorority sisters were constantly getting married as they graduated. I was really sad I couldn't make my LLLLS (Little

- Little - Little - Little Sis) Kori's wedding but I think she understood. One of the events I did make it to was a Chi O anniversary. Every five years they have something, and this year was one of those years. I wasn't happy and certainly wasn't "prosperous" or "successful", but I wanted to go to reconnect with my sisters.

What was interesting was that I had built a legacy. Once again, I would introduce myself and they would say "Oh you're Daisie". One of those people was a young beautiful black woman. She had heard stories of how I tried to introduce "culture" to Chi O. When I was a member, every week, as the Student Council Chairman for the Intercultural Relations committee I would invite my sisters to this or that event.

I was involved with every cultural group on campus including, SHPE (Society of Hispanic Professional Engineers,) NSBE (National Society of Black Engineers), ASU (Asian Student Union), etc... I was the organizer of the first Diversity Week, which I learned 15 years later was still going strong! My boyfriend was an Alpha (Alpha Phi Alpha) and some of my good friends were Deltas (Delta Sigma Theta) so I was always inviting my sisters to go to step shows and support the black Greeks. As a black-white woman, I was constantly in search of ways to fill my cultural needs, but I was also trying to teach the people around me that different was good. Difference meant growth. Difference meant knowledge (and good food). I supported Diwali festivals, step shows, pow-wows, and everything in between.

I am grateful that even though I left, the enthusiasm didn't leave. When I graduated from college, I had a small party and I invited Brother George. Brother George was not only the Alpha sponsor, he was also the University's Affirmative Action Director. I had always respected him and was glad when he showed up to the party with his wife. I was busy being the center of attention and the hostess at the party, but I did hear what he said to my mother... "Daisie came to UMR ready to change the World". I did and still believe that I can change the world and I am glad that I left that legacy.

Years later and hours after all the official ceremonies many of us are hanging out at some random sister's house when I met Sarah. Turns out

Sarah is only a few years younger than me, but I didn't know her when we were in school together. We got to talking and she was living in San Francisco at the time. Excited, I ask her, "That is one place I always have wanted to visit, do you mind if I come visit you?"

Like most people I know, she loves company and showing off her new home, so she says yes, and we exchange information. Less than a month later while making cold calls, a guy named Chris called me from CA and said the magic words "50% travel" and I was moving to San Jose, CA. I had never imagined myself living in CA because I had always imagined it as a potential island.

19

⌇

1989 (Craisiedaze's Version)

California had always seemed exciting but dangerous to me. California always had an air of mystery and 1989 was a monumental year in my memory. During the 1989 World Series, there was an earthquake in San Francisco. I was 13 and a huge baseball fan so I was watching the series in my uncle's living room when it happened. The death and destruction were devastating, and it left an impression on me. It seemed strange to me that something so horrific could happen during something as pure as the World Series.

I couldn't harp on it too long because just a few weeks later the Berlin Wall came down which meant the end of the Cold War. The Cold War had given me nightmares as a child and even with the celebrations, I was anxious and suspicious. Both these events happened after we had left the comforts of Kansas City and had moved in with my uncle and his family in Lawrence. It's an example of the "Devil You Know." I traded, not by choice, the Monster for life in a "college town" amid world and life-changing changes across the world.

Ten years later, I would be part of many Y2K plans and programs, but I think that the most life-altering changes happened 10 years earlier in 1989. We all lived through them, and most were unaffected, but they made a significant impact on our lives. In my case, it almost caused me not to move to CA, but the ridiculous salary and hint of travel reeled me in and encouraged me to make the leap.

20

Silicon Valley

Working for Motorola and then Flip Chip, I was very familiar with Silicon Valley. In our offices, there were posters everywhere with a map of Silicon Valley and all the companies that resided there. This was before the dot.com boom and bust so it was mostly chip manufacturers like Motorola, Intel, National Semiconductor, etc... There were also chip designers, computer manufacturers, and electronics companies. For a Tech Geek, Silicon Valley is heaven, and I was living there!

I worked next to Cisco and drove by Yahoo, eBay, and PayPal on the way to work. I had been laid off by both Flip Chip and the medical device company because I was "the last one in" so "I was the first one to go." When I started this job, I decided that I would come up to speed and become value-added as fast as possible so that I wouldn't be the first to go again. I jumped in feet first and loved it!

I was back in semiconductors, but I was on the other side of fab. This time I was a supplier, we built capital equipment used in the fabs. In my case, we were in metrology, measuring or defect detection tools. It was funny, during the interview for this position I remember one guy asking me over and over again how much I knew about certain systems, and I replied, "I don't know, I used it and if it broke I called you guys". Now I was one of "you guys." By this time, the new fabs were manufacturing

12-inch wafers, were completely automated, and were located predominately in Asia. My machine was on the cheap side at $4 million, our top-selling machines sold for over $20 million.

I was a New Product Introduction Engineer for the service side of the company, essentially the project manager for a new product. This meant that I had to be the expert of the machine which, considering its size and complexity, was an enormous task. In the line of command for our technicians, I was the next to last stop. Let me explain. In each fab we have CSEs — customer services engineers; regionally we have TSEs — tech support engineers; and then you get me. If I can't figure it out, we call the design engineers, which happens more often than I like to admit.

Being an NPI, or Project Manager was finally a perfect position for me. It is a very dynamic position, you work with several different departments, you are doing several different things simultaneously and it's constantly changing and evolving. I LOVED it!

21

⌖

Traveling for Work Take 2

Again, I was the only woman in the group, but I liked the people I worked with. My boss was a great guy and eventually one of my favorite bosses but at the beginning I was frustrated. He tended to feel like he had to "protect" me. The first year, he never sent me to the field and was always making excuses about how much he needed me onsite. Eventually, I became unglued, and I asked him about it. He said, "I don't want to set you up for failure." Of course, I didn't take this well but of course, I knew he meant well but it frustrated me to no end! First it was China, then Malaysia...I felt like I was a Motorola all over again. I was itching to travel and prove my worth!

I did my best to keep it low key though. I was busy both professionally and personally, so I was going with the flow. I was the NPI for two different machines and I was becoming the "stage" expert. The stage was what moved the wafer around. The microscope had to be stationary, so the wafer had to move. The wafer moved on a "stage" that moved in the X-Y direction. The microscope had limited Z direction. For all you non-geeks out there... X means in the east–west direction, Y means in the north-south direction and Z is three dimensional so the up and down direction.

There were a lot of problems with the stage. It was a legacy tool, meaning it was in a lot of our machines, (because we hadn't found a more accurate replacement) it was inaccurate at times and over time it got worse. The stages were sensitive, and you had to find their "sweet spot." Seriously, it was all about torque and blah blah blah, really it meant that I put in some numbers, ran a test, waited for the results, and tweaked it more. It often took hours to find that sweet spot and I was rapidly becoming one of the experts. It was actually a "stage" issue that finally took me to Japan and the beginning of a journey that I always knew that I was destined to embark on.

Years later, I would look back at pictures of myself and understand part of my boss's hesitation. I was 28 but I looked like I was 16. Kind of hard to get respect when you look like you barely graduated high school let alone college. As proud as I am that I don't look my age it certainly hasn't helped me professionally.

22

～

Game Plan for Life

In the meantime, I was living my life. Before I moved to San Jose, I was very involved with my church and the Life Teen program in Mesa, AZ. Before I even moved, I researched churches in the area that had a Life Teen program. I moved to San Jose on a Thursday and that Sunday I was in a church/parish that I would call home.

It had everything I was looking for. A Life Teen program, amazing youth ministers, and diversity! In Arizona, I was mostly working with "white" and "holier than thou" people. I never felt like either one of those, and it was hard to connect with some people. I was "real" and "ghetto" and the teens I ministered to had "real" problems. They were addicts, abused, troubled and ashamed. They came to me not because I was "holier than thou" but because I was "real." I grew up abused and poor. My mother and siblings were alcoholics and drug addicts. We spoke the same language. I didn't "force" my religion on them. I listened to them, cried with them, and prayed for them. For me, being Catholic was a choice that I made. I made it because I needed structure in my life, I admired the many Catholic women in my life and felt like it was home.

In AZ, the teens I ministered to were mostly cradle Catholics. Their parents made their decisions and they felt forced to be a part of a religion that didn't seem to help them. How could they be Catholic when their

"Catholic" father was physically, mentally, or sexually abusing them? Where was this god?

I totally got that because I prayed and prayed for pardon and rescue when I was being abused as a child. In Arizona, I was personally ministering to over 30 teens. I also got my two sisters and my youngest brother baptized and confirmed in the church. Religion and Faith aren't for everyone, but to me and my family, when we needed it, it provided comfort and strength. When my youngest sister got married in the Catholic Church to a wonderful man of God, she thanked me for introducing her to the church and I knew that I did God's work.

When I got involved with the church in San Jose it was different because I was once again the minority! Most of the teens were poor and a minority. I felt instantly at home! My teens were Vietnamese, Filipino, Black, and Mexican. Remember? I like being the center of attention and with this group I certainly was!

Don't forget though, I was a leader, a chaperone, a mentor. We were supposed to be not only leaders but examples. Well, I was obviously one of the sinners that Jesus would eat and drink with, but I was also hungry. I was hungry for inspiration, motivation, and for the future.

As a core member or leader of this organization, you would learn about something and then share it with the teens. One such lesson was called "The Game Plan for Life" by Lou Holtz, former Notre Dame Football coach. We spent an entire semester working through his book. The most astonishing thing in the book for me was the chapter about goals. Throughout my life I had heard about goals, making them SMART, writing them down, etc.... but what I found astonishing about his outlook on goals was that he said "categorize" them.

Don't just put...In Five Years I will....

Instead, write: My travel goals are... My professional goals are... My educational goals are...My family goals are... etc...

So that is what I did. I have since lost that journal, but I wrote goals for every aspect of my life. Educationally, I wanted a Masters degree. Professionally, I wanted to be a manager and help support other women. The longest list was my travel goals. Again, I don't have that journal on me, but I do remember that was number one – Paris and number 2 was Egypt. The list filled an entire page, and finally, in 2005, I was able to make my dreams and goals come true!

23

~

Finally Traveling for Work!

I can't remember if Japan was on my original list, but I have always been interested in Japan— the culture and of course the food! After so many trips that had fizzled and died, when I finally got the go-ahead to go to Japan to investigate a stage issue, I was ecstatic. We had spent a couple of days trying to help the team in Japan troubleshoot the problem via conference calls and emails but finally, it was determined that they needed someone onsite, and that someone was me. Unfortunately, it also meant another random technician. He was part of the engineering team and not the service team, so I didn't know anything about him. When I heard the news, I was instantly anxious. I had a feeling that there would be some "power play" but I didn't care too much because I was finally going somewhere!

To be honest, I was already frustrated by the Japan team. I would give them instructions and they wouldn't follow them. A lot of people, including my boss, would say that the problem was "language" so I would try asking in different ways, bullet points, more details over conference calls, etc....but it just wasn't working so I was on a plane. Unfortunately, they sent a babysitter with me.

The babysitter was an older white guy named Bob. We didn't have an admin that would make our flight and hotel arrangements so we would normally ask the local team for the logistics, and it was the same for this trip. We didn't sit together during the flight, but I made most of the other arrangements, including having the local team pick us up from the airport. Since the trip was so last minute, we had to pick up our domestic ticket at the airport in Nagoya and this is where I saw Bob's true self. Apparently, he had lived in Japan for a couple of years, so he was able to speak some Japanese. The thing about Japan is that it is mostly women in the service industry, and they all seem to be young and cute. Bob turned out to be a huge flirt so much so it was embarrassing because he flirted with everyone! I was very uncomfortable with him.

Our customer was Sony, and they were located in a small town outside of Nagasaki called Isahaya. It was so small that there weren't any major hotels so what we got was a workerman's hotel with just the basics. It wasn't the capsules you read about but compared to most hotels it was tiny. The bathroom was so small that my knees would knock on the wall when I sat down on the toilet and my head would hit the ceiling when I got into the shower.

When we checked into the hotel Bob, after way too much flirting, he asked me if I wanted a Japanese or Western breakfast. I wasn't sure, so I went with the Western. We had plans to meet the local team at 9:00 am in the lobby so I knew breakfast would be possible, but I didn't expect to wake up at 3:00 in the morning! Talk about jet lag! I somehow managed to go back to sleep but I still woke up early enough to have breakfast. I went down to the dining hall and handed the attendant my little square ticket that said I wanted the Western breakfast. Turns out it included eggs over easy, bacon, rice, orange juice, coffee, bread, yogurt, and a small salad. Well, I don't like eggs over easy, but I was hungry, so I ate the egg white part by cutting around the yolk. I ate just about everything else except for the bread and the orange juice. There is significance to this...so don't forget!

24

~

Respect...Never Given...Always Earned

This was my first official international trip, so I was super excited but also nervous because of the issue. It felt like a test, and I didn't want to blow it. Since Sony is a traditional company, the local team did all the talking. I just hung back because although I am a super talkative and a social person I had learned to just watch and observe when I'm in unfamiliar territory.

We started trying to diagnose the problem and after a while, I tried to make some suggestions, but I was continually ignored. There was only one chair, so my back had started to hurt from standing there, I was hungry, so I was almost to the point of getting bitchy, and I was irritated that no one was listening to me. I kept my cool, but I was relieved when Kato-san said he wanted to go to lunch. I think he finally let us go because he wanted to smoke, but I didn't care because I was glad to get out of the fab for a while. We had lunch and returned to the fab less than an hour later for much of the same.

Bob was leading the show even though I was the expert, and the Japanese team was listening only to him. After being in the fab for over

10 hours, we collected some data and called it a night. I was so exhausted that I almost turned down dinner, but I am glad I didn't.

Isahaya was so small that there weren't any big-name-brand restaurants. Most restaurants were hole-in-the-wall type places with at most 5 tables. There was one cool restaurant that had several rooms with long wooden benches that could hold maybe 10 people, but it was usually crowded. In all the restaurants, you take off your shoes and usually, you sit on a cushion on a bench or on the floor. In some cases, it would be a raised area where you could put your foot down into the center but in most cases, you sat cross-legged at the table.

In Japan, the first thing the waitress brings you is a hot towel to wash your hands with. It was nice to kind of wipe the day away. After the towels, the guys would just start ordering food. Usually, the menu was a bunch of characters written on a chalkboard or on posters on the wall. I never saw a menu so I just had to trust that I would get food I would like. Luckily, I LOVE food, so I was easy to please, but it turns out Bob was a vegetarian which doesn't work too well in Japan. I would see the Japanese guys roll their eyes, but they still tried to accommodate him. They asked us if we wanted a beer and we both declined. Him for religious reasons and me because I don't like beer.

In Japan, the food comes when it's ready. They would order a bunch of food and it comes when it's prepared. They only provided chopsticks, so I ate with chopsticks. This was one of the first things the team noticed. "Aww...Daisie-san, you know chopsticks?" Yes, I learned to eat with chopsticks growing up with my friends from Southeast Asia. That and I love Asian food, so I have been practicing. The next comment came after I had tried everything..." Daisie-san, you like Japanese food?" Yes! I love it! I responded to his question with, "You don't get to be this big without loving food in general." Which made everyone laugh. I learned that each person tries a little of each dish and once all the food is on the table you can really go at it. I learned that I had to ask, "Is there more food coming?" so I would know when to really start eating.

Did I mention that I was the only woman in the group? Did I mention I was the only woman engineer in the whole place? At this point,

I could tell that the guys were finally softening up to me. They were asking me more questions and telling me stories. The final straw though was when they ordered shōchu and I asked them to order me one as well. Shōchu is like vodka, it's made from potatoes. Sake is made from rice. They pretty much taste the same to me and I am not sure why this group preferred Shochu, but that is what they would drink after dinner over ice. I asked for lemon to squeeze over mine to give it a little more flavor. At this, the guys started talking in hurried Japanese and then asked "Daisie-san, you like Shōchu?"

"Sure, it tastes like vodka," I replied, and they all laughed. A bond was formed over good food and drinks.

The next day they finally started listening to me!! We had a long way to go but it was a start. Our days looked like this: have breakfast, conference call with the team in the US, back in the fab, and then dinner. Dinner was always family style which started with beer and ended with Shōchu. I tried everything! I found out that if I said "I like this. What is it?" it would show up again the next night. If I didn't comment they would ask me about it and I would give them my honest opinion. During this trip, I didn't find any food I didn't like. I just liked some things more than others and yes Kobe beef was one of my favorites.

Breakfast was pretty funny. The second day I got scrambled eggs, ham, rice, orange juice, coffee, bread, yogurt, and a small salad. I ate all the eggs and everything else except for the orange juice and bread. So, on the third day, I got eggs over easy, bacon, rice, coffee, yogurt, and a small salad. Wow, she was studying me. I didn't eat the yolk again so on the fourth day she said "scramble" and did a "scramble" motion by moving her closed fist in a circle. I said, yes "scramble" and ate scrambled eggs for the rest of my trip. I would visit Isahaya several more times over the next couple of months and she would always serve me the same thing. That was great customer service and memory!

25

~

A Good Catholic Girl

Workwise we were making a lot of progress but finally, they decided to take a break and give us Sunday off. Some of the guys had been working for two weeks straight and they needed a break. They invited me to go to the hot springs with them but that sounded like way too much TMI for me, so I opted to go to Nagasaki for the day. To be honest, I didn't remember that Nagasaki was the second nuclear bomb site. When I was researching what to do in Nagasaki for the day most of the activities included visiting sites that paid tribute to the bomb and peace, including the Peace Park.

Before I begin with that story, I want to tell you about accessing the internet in Japan at that time. It was a weird experience. I was usually in the fab and then with the Japanese team afterward, so I didn't have time to check email or "surf the web" and when I attempted to it was all in Japanese. Usually, I didn't have enough brain cells to try to figure it out but finally, on Saturday night, I had to figure it out. Somehow, I managed to find my way to some English sites and found a "day tour." I planned my day, I would start at the Peace Park, then walk to another place, and then another. I didn't have a printer, so I wrote it all down. I was supposed to go by myself via train but of course, the crazy gross old guy decided to come with me! UGH!

One stop on my day tour was a stop at a Catholic church so I thought I would head him off there. "Yeah, I am going to go to Mass first and then tour around". He was a Seventh Day Adventist so he decided to leave me to my faith but that was after walking me most of the way there. Babysitter much? YES!!

The walk was interesting though. Along the way, I would see different plaques talking about the bomb and its effects. It was spooky and humbling. I couldn't help but think "Do they hate me?"

By the time I had made it to the church, I knew that Mass was over because there was a stream of people leaving. I continued anyway. In southern Japan, there are lots of Christians due to the European trade. This church had been destroyed during the bombing and the only remaining item had been a statue's face of Mary. It was on display at the church, and I wanted to see it. Of course, since a single white woman is such an anomaly, many people approached me. I didn't really know what to do so I asked, "Is there another Mass?"

There weren't any more Masses at that church, so a guy drew me a map to the International Student Center where there was an English Mass. It's now about 10:50 and mass there started at 11:00 so I decided to attempt it. Who knows who I would meet? I tried to follow the directions and after about 20 minutes I got frustrated and was ready to quit when I saw a cab. I figured I would ask the cab driver where the center is and if he didn't know I would ask him to take me to the Peace Park. As I approached the cab an African family stepped out of the cab, so I looked around me and realized I had actually found the center. I followed the family into the building which included taking off our shoes exchanging them for sandals and walking up a gazillion steps. When we got to the top, we encountered a sign that said, "Mass delayed until 12:00". At this point I had options, I could leave because really, I didn't have to go to mass today, or I could stay. I decided to stay.

I followed the African family to a library of sorts where there were lots of people waiting. Besides the African family, it seemed like most of the people were Filipino. I settled in and we chatted. At one point a Japanese guy sat next to me and attempted a conversation. He attended English

Mass so he could practice English. To help him I asked the standard questions, "What do you study etc...?" After I had exhausted the normal questions I asked him, "Why was Mass delayed?"

He answered, "Because the pope died".

26

∽

A White Girl, A Vietnamese Woman, a Japanese Man, and a Mexican Priest

Walk into a bar... JOKE!

As I mentioned previously, I was pretty involved with my church at this time. I had plans to go to World Youth Day that summer to attend a Mass with Pope John Paul 2. He was a phenomenal man, priest, and Pope. I knew he was sick, but I had no idea that he had died. I didn't check English news and all the newspapers etc.... just showed pictures of the Pope. Again, I had no idea!! So, when this guy informed me of the death I was stunned and devastated but mostly I felt alone. I had built such a strong community at my church that the news was tough to deal with alone. Being Daisie though, I bowed my head, said a prayer, and moved on.

A little before noon we headed to the chapel which was at the top of the building. It was small, bright, quaint, and felt appropriate. While I searched for a seat a woman approached me and asked if I would read the second reading. It was obvious at this point that I was the only native English speaker and white person in the room. The reading was very powerful, and it took all my willpower not to cry while reading it. It was very appropriate for mourning the Pope.

The priest then read the gospel and gave his homily. It was then that I learned that he was Mexican by birth. I looked around at the audience which was Filipino, African, and Vietnamese and I realized I was home. The priest gave an amazing homily. He had been in Japan for over 20 years and had been a big part of every Japanese-Catholic movement there had been. He had met both Mother Theresa of Calcutta and Pope John Paul 2. He shared his stories with us which of course had us all crying.

After an emotional mass, we gathered in a break room for tea and coffee. I was starving at this point so all I had on my mind was food! Again, since I am the only native English speaker and white person, many people wanted to talk to me including a very pregnant Vietnamese woman and the Japanese guy I was speaking to before mass. Due to my hunger, I invited a few people to lunch but only the Vietnamese woman and the Japanese man accepted.

The Japanese man was working at a hotel and the Vietnamese woman named Minh had married a Japanese man who traveled and worked in Southeast Asia often. After she had gotten pregnant, she moved in with his parents in Nagasaki. She majored in English and spoke English but not Japanese. Her in-laws didn't speak English or Vietnamese. She was excited to speak English with someone and we hit it off instantly.

27

❧

Yes, They Have Electronic Toilets

The three of us agreed to go to lunch. We took the trolley/cable car, which was one of the day trip items to the restaurant. The restaurant was a family-style Japanese restaurant that reminded me of a Shoney's, and we all had a great time talking and laughing. As part of the conversation, we talked about Vietnamese food. She was surprised that I knew and liked the food and as we were leaving the restaurant she asked if I wanted to come over to her house for dinner. She wanted to make spring rolls, so of course I accepted her offer!

We went shopping for the ingredients and then headed up the hill to her house. I was excited to see a real Japanese house! I didn't get to see too much but I was surprised to see the same electronic toilet in the bathroom that they have in the hotels and businesses. Electronic toilets that warm the seat, has a bidet, and sings to you. Apparently, that is the norm there, well not everywhere, the other option was basically a hole in the ground which I always found hard to navigate aka keep my balance (especially when wearing jeans).

Dinner and preparation for dinner was entertaining. The mother-in-law actually knew a little English and she wanted to practice so we did. Minh asked if I wanted to help make the spring rolls so as I wrapped the rolls, the three of us chatted and had a good time. Eventually, dinner was ready, so the father-in-law came in to join us. The four of us ate pretty informally in the kitchen and, broken English aside, it was a great experience. After dinner, the father-in-law offered me Sake.

As I was waiting for the Sake, though, I made a mistake and complimented the tea set. I asked where I could buy a set and the next thing you know they were presenting me with a tea set. I accepted the gift, but I felt bad because although I did like the tea set, I was just trying to make conversation. After a few "shots" – not sure if they call them shots, they offered to take me to the train station. Minh and I kept in touch for at least a year after this experience including her sending me pictures of her baby which came two weeks later.

28

~

Take Advantage of Every Opportunity

That Sunday was a great experience but, of course, Monday rolled in and we got back to work again. Luckily we got everything settled by late Tuesday. Again, this was my first time in Japan, so I had to rely on Bob. He decided we were to fly out of Osaka, so I went with the flow. We took one of the express trains from Isahaya to Osaka and I really enjoyed the ride. I can't remember how long the ride was, but it was comfortable, easy, and fast. The train went so fast it kind of rocked you side to side. I had a book that I tried reading in between the stupid sexually charged and inappropriate commentary from Bob. I read and tried to ignore Bob. When we got to Osaka, at first I was underwhelmed. It was just another big city. The only difference was that the signs were in Japanese. Well except for the castle!

It turned out that the time I was in Japan was Cherry Blossom season. Different cities and provinces would have festivals at different times but to my luck, Osaka was knee-deep in theirs. After checking into the hotel, we went directly to Osaka Castle, one of the most remarkable structures I had ever seen. It was huge, menacing, and beautiful all at the same time. It was the past, the present, and the future all at the same time.

Osaka Castle had a moat and a large wall protecting it. The rocks that formed the wall were taller than me. I learned later that the castle I was looking at (and had been in awe of), was a reconstruction. There were some hints, such as an elevator on the side, but for the most part, it felt real, so real that it felt spooky as if there were ghosts or spirits about. The bitterness and disgrace was there, again only in feelings and emotions not by aggression. The exhibits weren't about WWII. They were about family history, their treasures, weapons, art, maps, and conquests.

In general, it was just a beautiful castle, and the grounds were even more beautiful with the cherry blossoms in bloom. Light pink flowers with a dark pink middle. I took pictures near the trees near the castle and on top of the wall. From there I could see all of the people who gathered to have a picnic under the new blooms. It was a beautiful sight, and I was glad that I got to be a part of it even if it was just a small part.

I left the next day via a train ride to the Osaka airport. It was a little stressful since it was my first time attempting this. Luckily the train announcements were in both Japanese and English, and I made it to the airport without incident.

29

∽

40/40

Not long after my trip to Japan, our second beta tool went to IBM in Fishkill, New York. Fishkill is a small town north of NYC off the Hudson River close to Poughkeepsie. I had never been to upstate New York and found it absolutely beautiful, it was springtime, so everything was green and majestic.

I was there to support the installation in case of any problems but it felt like a vacation (when I wasn't actually in the fab). At first, I was there with just the installation engineer, a cocky young guy who was cool but a little much at times. We would hang out during the week but when the weekend came I was off to NYC. It was over an hour away by train and I was there almost every weekend.

The first weekend I was there I just wanted to get to know the city and enjoy the weather. I dressed in jeans and a T-shirt, not bothering to be too cute since I was just going to be walking around and reading. I hung out in Washington Park and walked around most of the day. I didn't bother finding a restaurant because I just ate hotdogs, meat on a stick, and other street food.

Towards the end of the afternoon, I decided to stop in the 40/40 club. 40/40 was owned by rapper Jay-Z (this was 2005). I thought I would just drop by to check the place out and head home. Needless to say, that did not happen. It was super early, but the club was open. I sat at the bar with a couple of other random folks and started reading. Well, that didn't last too long because the bartender asked if we wanted to take a tour of the club.

We were downstairs which wasn't anything super special. There were some white chairs hanging from chains from the ceiling, a bar, and the dance floor. The upstairs is where the magic happened. There were several VIP rooms, and each had a different theme. There was a cigar room that looked like an old white guy's den but in a cool sexy way and a sports-themed room that had signed jerseys framed and hanging on the walls. Those are the only two rooms that I remember but I know there were more.

After the tour I sat and continued talking to the people at the bar, then more people joined us, and then even more. The next thing I knew I was surrounded by people, mostly men talking about who knows what. Then we started dancing and then it was after three o'clock in the morning and I missed the last train upstate.

I have only a couple of choices. Continue to party until the next train at 5 a.m., hang out in front of the train station, get something to eat, or take a taxi back. The choice was kind of made for me when a couple asked a taxi driver how much it would be to go upstate. We decided it would be cheaper if we split the fare. So off we went and $185 later I was home in my own bed with phone numbers from guys living in every burrow.

30

∾

It's Just Comedy

The next weekend was Memorial Day weekend, and I was back in the city. I had spent the week nights chatting with my various men and decided I only liked one of them so I met him for dinner in the city on Saturday night. It was pretty much a dud, so we left each other after dinner and I walked around Times Square. Memorial Day equals Fleet Week in NYC so there were tons of cute men walking around in their uniforms, so I was enjoying people watching.

If you have ever been to any major tourist city you know there are always people on the street trying to sell you stuff. I am usually pretty good at saying no but one of the salesmen was selling Improv tickets. I don't remember the deal, but I remember him saying "Black Comedy" night which of course piqued my interest. I almost said no when I realized that Black Comedy Night was on Sunday nights, but then I remembered I didn't have to work on Monday. Score!

I headed back to Fishkill, but I was back the next night for the show. Again, I was just wearing jeans and a T-shirt, nothing too cute. I had asked one of my many men, why he was interested in me, and he said because I "smiled." I didn't think much of it until I realized that yeah, no one in New York smiled.

The NYC Improv has several levels and theaters, and the Black

Comedy Night was in the basement, so down I went. I started to hand the guy my ticket when he said, "Comedian's that way..." and pointed to the door at the end of the hall. I laughed and said, "Not a comedian." I mean, really? What part of me looks like I would be a part of Black Comedy Night?

Still laughing to myself, I decided to sit by myself to the right of the stage. The setup was funny here. The stage was in a corner and the seats were either right in front of the stage or to the right and back. No one was sitting to the right, so I got a great seat at the end of the table with an unobstructed view. Like always, I was super early, so I sat back to people watch. To my joy, most of the patrons were military but to my disappointment, they were mostly white. I resigned myself that I wasn't going to find any new men that night, well that was my thought until a super cutie sat down across the table from me. It was obvious that he was way too young for me, but I played along anyway. Turns out he was a promoter for the local hip-hop radio station, KISS "something". We chatted for a while, and he gave me a couple of tickets for the concert on Monday. I didn't have the heart to tell him I couldn't make it, so I took them and gave them away later that night.

If I remember correctly, the comedians were three black men and one Puerto Rican woman. No one was a big name, but I laughed a lot and had a great time. During one of the breaks, the MC called two men on stage for a contest. They had to call out a basketball team back and forth until someone couldn't go on anymore. It was surprising that they really didn't know many teams. During the next break, they called for two women so of course I volunteered, and I was chosen. Our contest was "Clothes Designers" and at first, I was bummed. I am not a designer brand person so I didn't think I could compete. I surprised myself and the crowd though. I think I started with Phat Farm, then FUBU, then Apple Bottom...or who knows. The MC turns to me and says, "Where did you grow up". I answered, "The Ghetto". The crowd laughed and I won the contest and got a goody bag full of prizes.

After the show, I was walking out when the Puerto Rican comedian who was hanging out with the other comedians on the stairs called out to me, "Hey white girl from the ghetto!" I laughed and said yeah that was me! She says, "Girl you cracked me up with that shit, wanna go hang out with us?"

Are you kidding? Hell yeah! So, the five of us hit the local clubs. I don't remember most of it, just that it was insane, and we hung out in places that didn't look like clubs. We drank, danced, and laughed a lot. Around 1 a.m., I realized I needed to catch the train or be stuck in the city again.

31

⁓

4th of July with the FBI, the State Department, and the Secret Service

The next couple of weeks passed with no excitement on the weekends. I think there were some problems with the installation which of course stressed me out and, if I remember correctly, it was cold and rainy. The next thing I knew, a month passed and it was the 4th of July weekend. I decided to head to Washington DC to see my friend JL. I had never been to DC before, and I was excited to see all the sites. My friend JL's husband had decided a couple of years before that he wanted to be an FBI agent, and he made it in. He was out of training and was based in DC. I looked into either taking the train or flying to get to DC, but the train made more sense. It was more cost-effective, and I think the timing worked better because they both were working.

JL met me at the station, then we made a quick stop at their apartment. After that, we headed to Maryland. Her sister-in-law and her husband lived on the water, and we were going to spend the weekend there. As we arrived, several others did as well, and it became way more exciting than I thought it would be. Turns out that when you live in DC and are married to an FBI agent, all of your friends are in that game. Everyone but maybe three of us was carrying. Needless to say, I felt very safe but also very in awe! One of my dreams had been to be a badass bitch carrying a gun. I still have that dream, but I am afraid I can't run after the bad guys.

Besides being in a house surrounded by young men and guns, we spent a lot of time in the water and visiting nearby Annapolis. We watched the fireworks on a pier while smoking chocolate cigars. It was an awesome experience participating in a 4th of July celebration so close to our capital. You could feel the history surrounding you even from the suburbs in Maryland.

The day after the 4th of July, we returned to DC where we only had time for one museum. The Native American museum had just opened a few months earlier so that's where we headed. It was really weird having to check in with security as we entered due to the gun, but after that, it was nothing but an amazing experience. The museum was beautifully built, and the plan was to rotate the exhibits every two years so that every native tribe of the Americas was showcased. Years later, I would visit the museum again with my cousin's son who is half Navajo.

Learning about the atrocities that the white man brought while exploring the New Worlds made me sick to my stomach but that's the whole point of that museum and of the holocaust museums and other like museums around the world. Highlight the things that people did wrong in the past so that we don't do that again! George Santayana's quote "Those who cannot remember the past are condemned to repeat it" comes to mind as I say that.

The trip was too short and unfortunately, JL and her husband didn't stay in DC for too long, so I wasn't able to visit them again there.

32

～

Fishkill Killer Reading Bees

The second half of my trip after DC was eventful but not in the way I thought it would be. I ended up going back to CA for a while but found myself in NY for round two. This time I was there to help solve a problem. The installation was over and now we were maintaining the system. We had trained the Customer Service Engineer and had a Tech Support Engineer there as backup but of course, there was a problem with the stage, so they called me.

The Tech Support Engineer was an Indian guy named Suni. He was new to the team and, since I was Curious George, I was always asking him questions. He was a Sikh from Punjab, like the Indian guy in Annie. They wear turbans have long beards (if you get to see them) and have other cool characteristics. We had spent some time together working in the lab back in San Jose but as always the trip to NY was an opportunity to *really* get to know each other. While in San Jose, I asked him if I could ask questions and he was ok with it that was how I found out he was Sikh and from Punjab. He was great about telling me about his faith and sharing about his culture. In New York, over trials on the machine and dinner, I learned even more about him and grew to respect him even more. Later in the year, he would invite me to the Sikh temple to celebrate one of their holidays. I felt honored to be invited.

While we were dealing with our problems, another machine was being installed and a good friend of mine, Corey, was working on that one. This time around, there were about six of us in Fishkill, so it was a little more entertaining. Instead of eating alone and calling one of my many men, I spent most of my time with my coworkers. We were staying at a Residence Inn since we were all there for so long and they had a great happy hour/snack service for when we got off of work. I was actually on my way down to one such event when I was stung by a bee for the first time in years.

The Residence Inn we stayed in did have a lot of flowers. It was summer, and it was semi-close to a creek, but I was still surprised to be stung. I ended up heading to IBM because I didn't know where else to go and all of a sudden I was surrounded by six people, my upper arm was swelling like crazy, and it was hot to touch. I had been stung by bees and wasps all the time as a child and I knew I wasn't allergic, but I started to freak out. Was it hard to breathe? Well now that you are asking...maybe? Oh and did I mention the six people were all hot young men? I don't even like white men, but these guys looked like they stepped out of a Fireman Hottie calendar. Hell, I probably couldn't breathe because their fine asses were there.

After what seemed like forever, they finally let me go back to the hotel. I got back, headed to my room, and then on my way back down to meet the team, I was stung again!!

Are you kidding me?? Seriously, true story! I ran back into my room, called the hotel management, and started crying. They advised cold compress with ice and...blah blah blah... all I am thinking is — *you can never leave the room.* I am now terrified to take even one step outside of my room. I took a photo of my arm which was now three times the size it normally was; it was bright "I stayed out in the sun too long" red and throbbing. I sent it to my boss and called him crying "I want to go home!" He, of course, laughs and tells me to suck it up. Needless to say, I did suck it up because I am a badass bitch...even if I don't have a gun.

The next day, Corey invited me to a movie since we had some downtime. We go and watch whatever, but I am constantly distracted by the throbbing in my arm and the thousand-degree sunburn I got when that bitch of a bee stung me. Every day after that day from hell, I would cautiously leave the hotel, terrified of bees but was never stung again. Later when I looked back on that day I realized that I was wearing a purple shirt that had a picture of a skunk on it and it said "Flower" – a Bambi reference. I guess it was my own damn fault. I was a Daisie who wore a Flower shirt. Who knew that bees could read?

33

~

No Regrets

As I mentioned previously, I had plans to attend World Youth Day (WYD) to see the Pope. It was 2004 when I originally signed up for the trip. I hadn't been in CA long, and I was still digging myself out of debt but after mass one night I was thinking to myself, "I could die tomorrow and be out of debt or I could die tomorrow and know that I had met the Pope". It was that thought that led me to sign up to be a chaperone for this trip. Again, I didn't want to live with regrets. There was so much about my life that I was already regretting.

Besides regret, I carried a lot of guilt around. It was really hard to be the only person in the family making money and my family thought that the "Bank of Daisie" was always open, and they could take from it whenever they wanted. When they weren't asking me for money they were blaming me for everything!!! Daisie did this...Daisie did that...

It didn't matter what was real, the only thing that mattered was what they thought and how I interpreted it. This of course was with extreme guilt. I have always had the "Save the World Complex," but I would (and still do) feel guilty because I can't even save my own family. I decided to put myself before my family and take this trip. The trip was over $3000.00 and it was the most amount of money I had ever spent on one trip and a non-tangible item. Sure, a car or a house, but a vacation? To me, this was unheard of and also uncomfortable. I felt guilty about doing something only for me. Sure, I had taken vacations and trips before, but not at this cost. It was so expensive that I didn't even tell my mom I was doing it. This was part of the advantage of distance.

That's not to say that paying for the trip was easy. When I was working with St. Tim's in Arizona, I didn't stress about money. It was a white middle-class church with a few others sprinkled in. The owner of the Arizona Cardinals was a parishioner, other business owners and athletes were also parishioners.

When I moved to San Jose, I chose a church that was the exact opposite of St Tim's and more like what I grew up with. The Filipino, Mexican, and Vietnamese communities are communities that lived and worshipped together and had the same values. Communities that want their children to grow up in peace. Parents sacrificed so that their children could live the American dream and be educated. I saw the same love and dedication in the eyes of these families that I had seen growing up.

Since most of the families couldn't afford the trip we did a ton of fundraisers throughout the year. I would make periodic payments, but I also participated in every fundraiser I could to support the teens. I didn't mind the work, but I was frustrated that not everyone participated and that some of the teens/families felt like they were "entitled" and didn't have to work that hard. That was frustrating but we managed to raise enough money to send everyone.

34

❧

WYD2005 - France

WYD2005 was in Cologne, Germany but we spent the week before the big event traveling to other Catholic sites. We were a group of 26, the youngest was 12 and the oldest was 70. We flew into Paris and immediately boarded a bus for Lourdes, France. This was after my disastrous attempt to speak French. I had taken French in high school and college but had never really gotten a chance to use it. I was so nervous that instead of saying in French "Do you speak English?" I said, "I speak English." Luckily the lady at the airport was nice and didn't make fun of my mistake. This of course made me more reluctant to try my bad French again.

Lourdes was the birthplace of Saint Bernadette, a young woman who had visions of the Virgin Mary; and a place where the water is said to have healing powers. We arrived at the camp, had dinner, cleaned up, and then headed to an outdoor midnight Mass. The entire area was lit up with candles and hundreds of people attended. It was beautiful and powerful but we were all exhausted from the trip so we probably didn't appreciate it as much as we should have.

The next morning, and every morning afterward in France, we had croissants with hot chocolate. The croissants were served with butter, cheese, and Nutella. The teens really loved the Nutella, but I didn't like the nutty flavor. After breakfast, we headed to the cathedrals and churches of Lourdes. We had Mass and then were given time to explore the area and visit the baths if we wanted. My small group consisted of young adults and Mama Linda. We called all the older Filipina women, "Mama". We explored the many churches and museums before we headed to the baths. Our timing was good because there wasn't a long line. I think we only had to wait about 30 minutes, but it was an easy wait. They had benches for the line which was nice for all of us since it was really warm, and we had been walking a lot. While in line, we could hear someone praying the Rosary over the loudspeakers and there were copies of the prayers in different languages.

The baths were interesting; they are said to have healing powers, but I wasn't really in need of healing. (On a side note, my back is killing me as I write this, maybe I should have asked for healing for my back.) The baths were scary but awesome at the same time. There were awesome attendants to help you. You change into a towel, and they help you step into the (freezing) water and then they pray with you. I asked for healing for my sister Maisie and other women who want children. They then help you change discretely into a dry towel, and you change back into your clothes which, by some miracle, don't get wet.

That night was one of the most beautiful moments of my life. One hundred thousand people from all over the world walked in a candlelight procession praying the Rosary in five different languages. It was another example of how powerful faith can be and how universal the Catholic Church is. Regardless of the language we all were united. To some people that may sound way too sentimental and religious but for me it was what I needed to be grounded and healthy.

The next day we headed back to Paris where we stayed in a hotel with an elevator so small that only two people and their suitcases could go up. Some of us took the stairs.

Paris was a dream come true! We started with Mass at Notre Dame and then explored other small churches and chapels in the area including St. Chapelle where they kept the Crown of Thorns. We then headed to The Daughters of Charity convent, but they were closed for lunch, so we went to lunch where I finally had Croque Monsieur and the teens had papas frites. While we were waiting for the convent to open, we were hanging out on the street and a gypsy walked by asking for money. We didn't give her money, but someone had some leftovers, so they gave them to the gypsy. The gypsy opened the bag, took a look, and handed it back. I guess she wasn't that hungry after all.

The Daughters of Charity is home to the creator of the Miraculous Medal, Saint Catherine Laboure. The incorruptible body of Saint Catherine is on display at the convent. Incorruptible means that the body, even after over 150 years has not decayed and is considered a miracle. Pretty awesome!

That night we went to the Eifel Tower where most of us walked the 710 steps to the second level. (To go to the very top, you had to pay to take an elevator.) Just getting that far was quite an accomplishment and it was an amazing view. It reminded me of how big the world around us is and how small we are.

35

～

Ciao Bella!

The next morning, we took the Paris subway to where we were meeting our shuttle bus. We were very obvious tourists, but I think that since we were such a diverse group we didn't get hassled like other groups did. Some groups got heckled on the subway, but we/I had a different experience. Just as we were getting off the subway a random black man, with the most beautiful French accent grabbed my arm and said, "You are beautiful". Wow! Well, that was certainly a good sendoff!

We flew into Rome and headed to our hotel, Hotel California, which seemed very fitting. After we checked into the hotel, we got the real tourist treatment as in paying a ridiculous amount of money for bottled water that was served during dinner. After dinner, we went to the Trevi fountain.

There was only one person in the entire group who was the same age as me, her name was Cristella and luckily, she was in my group. We had met the previous year on a retreat and had hit it off immediately. She was an amazing woman, who had gotten pregnant and married young and then subsequently divorced. Her ex-husband abused her, but she had the courage to leave him when her daughters were still young. She finished high school and then college and was working full-time to support her kids. I admired her courage and determination. She deserved this vacation, and I was glad to be a part of the journey with her.

After hanging out at the Trevi fountain for a while and throwing our coins in (of course backward) most of the group broke up to find gelato. Cristella and I headed out to find a drink but what we found was lots of little cafes. It was a nice night, so we decided to sit outside and enjoy a cup of coffee. We asked for decaf, and the waiter laughed at us. Cristella and I looked at each other and decided to go for the coffee but we added a shot of Baily's liquor to both. We figured the liquor would counter the effects of the coffee.

HA!! At one o'clock in the morning, I hear Cristella whisper, "You awake?" "Yeah," I reply.

Then again at two o'clock and again at three o'clock, we both tossed and turned for hours only to have to wake up early. To make matters worse, this was the busiest day of our whole trip. We (the entire group) practically ran to the Vatican for Mass the following morning. Mass was in the crypts, which wasn't as creepy as I thought it would be. On the way into one of the chapel areas, we passed by the crypt of John Paul II. It was surreal.

After Mass, we headed back upstairs for a tour of St. Peter's Basilica. The tour started with Michelangelo's Pietà, one of his first statues and the only one he signed. It's the one where Mother Mary is holding the body of the crucified Jesus. The details were amazing, and it was breathtaking. From there we learn that just about everything in the Basilica is an optical illusion. The paintings are mosaics and the letters in the dome all look the same size, but some are over 6.6 ft high. We learned that St. Peter was buried in this spot, and this is why they built the church here.

The tour was amazing, and we learned a lot. It is a remarkable place and not just for Catholics. There is a lot of history and art there. After the tour, we were able to walk around even more and pray. Cristella and I tried not to fall asleep on our feet.

36

Silencio!

After the tour, we all met at the obelisk in front of the Basilica and broke off for lunch. There were a ton of super cute little cafes surrounding the Vatican and my group and I settled right in. I can't remember what I ordered but I remember what Cristella ordered because the second they put it in front of her she freaked out. She had ordered a shrimp pasta dish not expecting whole shrimp, heads and all. Of course, I couldn't let the shrimp go to waste and Mama Linda couldn't let the shrimp heads go to waste. Poor thing didn't order shrimp for the remainder of our trip.

After lunch, we went to the Vatican museums where the Sistine Chapel is. We were told we only had an hour to explore the museum, so my group speed-walked through the other exhibits. We kept hearing that there was a shortcut to the Sistine Chapel, but we never found it, the shortcut that is. Even walking at that speed, it took us 45 minutes to find the Chapel. It was very different from what you see on TV. It was dark, and of course, filled with tourists, it was also filled with Swiss guards who seemed to be constantly shouting "Silencio" to everyone. It was frustrating because I wanted to explain the significance of the paintings etc., to my group. To be honest it wasn't the first or the last time someone would shout "Silencio" at me. Seems I was always in trouble.

Since we couldn't talk about what we were seeing and we couldn't take pictures, we just left and rejoined our group at the obelisk. Of course, since I hate being late, we were one of the first groups back, so we waited.

37

~

The Hunger Games - Roman Style

Once we were all rounded up, we boarded the bus and went to the Coliseum (Colosseum in Italian), home of the Roman Hunger Games, also known as the Gladiatorial Games. It was a massive structure and unlike most discovered ruins, most of it hasn't been rebuilt. They have secured it enough so that you can walk around safely but most of it was the original stones, very little had been restored. This included the ground level which didn't have a top so you can see the tunnels that ran underneath the ground. This is where they kept the surprises like lions, tigers, crazy gladiators, etc....

After a few laps around, there really wasn't too much to look at and we were given lots of time to explore but it had already been a long hot day so a group of us found a shaded spot and relaxed. I was always buying books at each site, so I read aloud to the group some interesting facts about the Vatican and the Coliseum. What I wanted to do was take a nap (which is what several other people did) but I was the leader, so I just read until it was time to tour the Forum located next to the Coliseum. The Forum was cool! There was just enough remaining to imagine what it looked like back in the day. Our tour guide was knowledgeable about the site and led us on a journey through time.

38

~

You Will Be Christian!

While on this whirlwind of a tour, I was reading Dan Brown's Angels and Demons, not knowing it was based in Rome when I first picked it up. It was pretty cool to be reading it and visiting the places in the book at the same time. I looked at every fountain, obelisk, and statue in a new light. The next day in Rome, we explored other really cool places including several churches that I can't remember the names of. I was keeping a journal at the time, but unfortunately, I lost it. However, so much was happening in one day and everything happened so fast that I couldn't write everything down.

What does come to mind is the Pantheon; it was created before the birth of Christ and was used as a temple to "gods." Of course, when the Christians found it they christened it and made it Christian, like they did with many structures in Rome. What was super interesting about this structure was the dome roof and how the building itself is an engineering miracle. I loved the story about how they built it. They filled the building with dirt and then shaped the concrete dome over the dirt. After it was dry and sturdy, they told the local people that they had hidden gold coins in the dirt. That place was cleared out within hours. Of course, there are more highly technical details about the structure, but I really liked their imaginative way of getting people to help.

Another memorable attraction was the *La Bocca della Verità* (the Mouth of Truth) where legend has it that if you lied and stuck your hand in the mouth it would be bitten off. Not that I am a huge liar or anything, but I wasn't about to stick my hand in its mouth!

39

～

Miracles (St Francis of Assisi)

One of my favorite quotes is "Preach the Gospel at all times and when necessary, use words." It has been attributed to St Francis of Assisi and I have tried to live by them. I want people to see Christ in me, my actions, and my deeds. Visiting Assisi and the surrounding areas was an amazing experience. The churches were beautiful, the pottery amazing, the people friendly, and the scenery spectacular. The church where St Francis had his vision of Christ was smaller than my room and now sits inside an even larger church (Our Lady of the Angels if I remember correctly...aka Los Angeles).

St. Francis is the patron saint of animals in general but most especially doves. We visited the Basilica of St. Francis while we were there and one of the miracles, we witnessed was a statue of St Francis that is always accompanied by at least two white doves. Isn't that awesome? Well, maybe you had to be there?

It was here in Assisi, after witnessing the miracles of the incorruptible bodies and the doves that we had to perform a minor miracle ourselves. We had been traveling together for over a week now and even the Mamas were bickering. Everyone was complaining, tempers were flaring, and morale was just down in general. A couple of us leaders got together and talked about what we should do. The organizers of the group were musicians and of course, were accompanied by a guitar. We decided to have a little prayer and washing of the feet session.

With Nelson singing in the background, our priest led us in prayer and then in the washing of the feet. Washing of the feet is a very humbling and emotional experience, especially when it's done spontaneously and not part of a service. My first experience with this happened at my first core retreat in AZ. The two youth ministers at the time started by washing everyone's feet and then a few people took turns washing other's feet.

The idea is to wash the feet of a person you have Ill will or thoughts about. In this case, I was so new I didn't think badly about anyone, but I did have a feeling that one person in the group didn't like me. I felt her animosity when I was around, but I ignored it. I figured I "can't please everyone..."

I was shocked when she grabbed my hand and brought me to the center of the room to wash my feet. I was shocked for MANY reasons. One of them was, the day before a few of us were talking about feet (in regard to getting pedicures), and this girl, let's call her Shawna, said that she hates for people to touch her feet, she doesn't even touch her own feet if she can help it. So, when she not only touched my feet but washed them, I was speechless. Well, if you don't count crying. I knew how much of a sacrifice it was for her and I was touched.

Something similar happened in Assisi. I didn't have a problem with anyone but apparently I was rubbing some people the wrong way. Turns out one of the married couples in our group was feeling jealous of my relationships with the teens, young adults, and Mamas. In general, I am loving, loud, crazy (as in "You so Crazy...Daisie"), and fun to be around so that attracts a lot of people to me. I knew this was a pilgrimage and we were there to be closer to God, but I was there to have a good time too! Well, I guess this ticked them off so once again I was in the center of the circle crying as one by one, they washed my feet. Like with Shawna, this cleared the air, and we became closer after this experience.

I think it helped the entire group. The next day we all had more energy and they complained less. It was a miracle!

40

⌒

½ Kilometer More!

As I mentioned, I speak a little French, and one young adult spoke a little more than I did. Another young adult could speak a little Italian and it turned out that if you spoke Spanish to the Italians they could understand you. This was helpful since half our group spoke Spanish. The only problem is - they answered in Italian! One of the funnier moments of our lack of language skills was when Cristella was calling home. As I mentioned she was a single mom so she would try to call home often, which almost always was a trial. Sure, we had a phone card, and the instructions were in both Italian and English, but the operators weren't. After about three tries to get it to work; Cristella cries out "Stop speaking Italian to me!" That was years ago, and we still crack up about it. That and how Cristella would say to me, "I am taking him home with me," when she spotted a cute guy (or Swiss Guard in tights). What she meant was...I am taking him home with my camera. Aww...the memories!

When we arrived in Cologne, Germany we realized that none of us spoke German. Luckily the event (World Youth Day) was very well planned, and they had tons of volunteers who spoke different languages, so we didn't have too many problems. Also, the events throughout the week were usually by language. For example, they had several opening Masses around the area. We chose to go to the English Mass for obvious reasons. Since so many countries speak English even as a second language it was usually the largest venue. We always had only some idea of where to go and how to get there (this was before smartphones and Google Maps) so we started towards the stadium. We would ask for directions, and they would always say, "Only ½ a kilometer more"! We walked and walked and walked. My group was almost always last because I had Mama Linda with me and although she had a ton of energy and stamina, she had very short legs and of course, we were late to mass. We were so late that we weren't admitted to the stadium and instead watched the Mass via the big screens set up outside.

41

~

Trains in Germany

After all the walking (at least 10 - ½ kilometers more) we were too tired to walk back to the hotel. We put the mamas in a taxi (Mercedes of course since we were in Germany) and we caught a train. When we first got on, we were fine, but then more and more people jumped on. When the doors finally shut, we were so squished it was hard to breathe. There weren't any windows, just narrow slits at the top of the cars. I am sure that you have heard that Europeans don't wear deodorant. Well, I don't know if it was that they don't wear it or that it was wearing off, regardless it was funky in there. I tried breathing into my shirt because the Irishman next to me smelled really bad. We couldn't even talk about them because they spoke English as well.

So here we were, squished in a hot and stinky train with a loud German man yelling over the loudspeaker. It was scary!! Of all places in the world, I did not want to be in a train with a scary German man yelling at me. German is such a harsh language, even when they are saying nice things it sounds mean. To make things worse, we weren't moving. We would go a couple of feet (meters maybe) and then stop. Like I said there was no air so some of the blokes (Irish term for guys) tried to open the door. It didn't open. I was standing pretty close to the door and watched this happen. They were getting angrier and more frustrated, and I was afraid they would start pounding on the door, so I got out of the way. To try to calm matters down someone started singing and soon just about the whole car was singing. Not sure how long we were in the car but when they finally made an official stop and opened the doors, most of us got off. Walking was much better than being crammed in a train with angry Germans yelling at you and crazy Irish men trying to escape. (Yes, the last part of that sentence was overly exaggerated, but it felt like that at the time...)

42

~

Papa Ratzi and the Angel

Cologne, Germany wasn't quite what I expected. Besides the incident on the train and Europeans not knowing how to form a line, our experience was pretty normal. The events of World Youth Day were held in several cities around that part of Germany including Dusseldorf. We learned more about our faith and each other. We worshipped, prayed, sang, danced, laughed, and cried.

The final event was an overnight vigil where we had adoration and slept; then it ended with Mass with the pope. After John Paul 2 died, Benedict, the 16th was chosen to lead the church. His real name is Joseph Ratzinger, so everyone called him Papa Ratzi (get it?). He is from Germany so of course the Germans (especially those from the Bavaria region) were super excited he was there. This was his first big event – like his introduction to the world. Pope JP2 (as his friends liked to call him) strongly believed in the Youth and started WYD celebrations in 1986. Pope Benedict wasn't as dynamic as JP2 was but praying in adoration with over 200,000 people and then having Mass with over 1 million people was an unforgettable moment.

As I mentioned we "slept" in the field between adoration and mass. Well, "sleep" didn't come easily. At first several of the groups around us were singing and dancing for most of the night. We joined in but after a while, even the teens couldn't hang anymore. Several people started getting sick including Cristella and after a couple of hours, she had a fever. One of the male chaperones had to go back to the hotel because he was so sick. The rest of us hung in there though. Most of us didn't have sleeping bags because we were told it would be hot. We slept on the ground with no pads, so it was uncomfortable, to say the least. After a while, it got really cold, so several of us tried to bundle together to keep warm. That didn't work very well though because it was so uncomfortable, we (really meaning me) tossed and turned a lot. I remember laying there trying to figure out if I should just get up and walk around when I felt an angel approach. I opened my eyes and all I saw was white...

Teresa our angel had gone to the first aid tent and came back with blankets!! We wrapped ourselves up in blankets and somehow managed to get at least a couple of hours of sleep.

43

Getting Screwed in Amsterdam

Almost immediately after mass, we left for the Netherlands. We stayed at a cool campsite outside of Amsterdam where we decompressed and reflected on our experience. We were all exhausted and ready to go home but we found the strength to share stories of our experiences with each other. Everyone from the twelve-year-old to the seventy-year-old had been touched and had grown in their faith. It was touching and reaffirming.

After that amazing experience, we got some much deserved and needed sleep and headed to Amsterdam. Wish I could say I saw something besides the airport but that wouldn't be true. Most of us still had some Euros left so we tried to spend most of them in the gift shops. I thought it would be fun to get nice lighters for my brothers and cousins (they are smokers). They were pretty expensive too – I think about 15 Euros so almost $20. Well apparently US Customs didn't like them and confiscated them ALL!! I was so bummed. Not just because of the money but also because I didn't have any other gifts for them.

Ok so maybe it wasn't Amsterdam that screwed me - damn US Customs!!

44

~

It's ALIVE!

A month later I was back in Japan. Our installation team was installing two new systems and of course, they ran into a stage problem. I was on a plane the next day but this time without the old guy. I did have a tiny incident in customs when they saw that I had recently returned from Amsterdam. No body-search, but they certainly checked and double-checked my luggage. It was a church trip! I promise!

One of the installation engineers was my roommate. She was a super cute Filipina woman named Pauline. She was younger than me but the oldest of like eight kids, so we had the whole "we're responsible for everyone" thing going on. She traveled a lot, so she was the perfect roommate.

Anyway, so she and the young guy, Greg, from New York were in Japan installing two systems. I got there, did some tweaking, and collected some data on the system. I decided to collect the same data on the second system the next day, so we went out to eat. By now, the local team knew me so I could call the shots and we were not stuck in the fab forever. That night we headed to a typical little Japanese place. It's a place where instead of sitting cross-legged on the floor, we are sitting on a raised bench, and we can place our legs in a hole under the table. (Sorry it's hard to explain) This is great because you can switch from being cross-legged when your legs go numb and let your legs hang. Still not super comfortable since there's no back support but it's better than getting stuck crossed-legged for hours.

As before there were no English menus, so the guys ordered the food. One of the dishes brought was sashimi, the head of the fish was pointed straight up from the plate like it was looking at the ceiling and the body was fileted in thin strips of meat beside it. As usual, as soon as the dish was sat down several of us reached over with our chopsticks to grab a piece. As we did so, though, the head starts breathing! The mouth opened to get air and you could see the gills open and close. Pauline was so shocked she fell out of our table cubby!

Between the fish and Pauline, we couldn't stop laughing. Who knew that the head of the fish wouldn't know it was dead? It took a few more breaths and then stopped. We continued eating after we got Pauline back to the table. Turns out this was a typical joke they like to play on white people. They pick the fish from a tank knowing it will not only be fresh but still alive! HAHA, the joke was on them. The white people just laughed, the Filipina was the one who freaked out!

In case you are wondering the head didn't go to waste. After that magnificent show, the fish then performed its last act by becoming miso soup.

45

~

Flood Alert

The next day was Friday, and I wasn't looking forward to working on the weekend. I tackled the stage problem and luckily was able to solve the problem within a few hours. Of course, it was then time to celebrate! I think Pauline and Greg hadn't planned on working the next day, so we stayed out pretty late. We almost went to a Hostess Bar with the guys but when I heard I had to pay to get in I decided not to. Maybe I should have, it would have been an interesting experience.

I don't remember much about the night, but I do remember switching to Gin & Tonics and arguing with Greg about Japanese culture. He was so adamant about something I was doing but I was thinking "When did you become the Japanese culture expert?" Oh, and the Japanese guys who were with us were also like – "Really?" They weren't offended and it was a ridiculous conversation. Pauline and I went back to the hotel (late and tipsy) and the guys headed to the hostess bar.

Super early the next morning, I woke up to the sound of the hotel phone ringing. It's Pauline and she tells me a story I cannot believe. Apparently, while we were out on the town the night before a small (tiny) water meter on our tool cracked and leaked. This tiny leak caused massive water damage in the subfloor of the factory. Several machines close by were shorted out including ours. No big deal except that the fab makes a million dollars of chips a day and this caused a major delay.

Luckily, Saturday morning in Japan means Friday afternoon in the US. A dozen conference calls later, I turned off my phone and fell back to sleep. Not much I could do but it was an entertaining story, and I wasn't to blame. Talk about design failure!!.

46

_∽_

I Have Ten Kids?

I love being the center of attention and training people is one of the aspects I loved about my job at the time. I not only got to be the center of attention, but I was in charge, I was the expert! This is important to me because there were so many aspects of my life where I felt like a five-year-old or a clueless teenager. When I am training people, I know that I am in charge, the expert, the boss, la jefa, and my self-esteem is strong and complete. There are very few situations in life, especially when dealing with my family where I am that self-confident.

One of my favorite experiences was working with our new Technical Support Engineers (TSEs) and Customer Service Engineers (CSEs) from China, Korea, and Singapore. Our sales guys, in all of their infinite wisdom, always tried to identify where our products could potentially end up and then asked us to train local CSEs. We had a training facility in Livermore, CA where the latest and greatest machine was located. At the time we would host a 5–6-person training class for 6 - 8 weeks. The trainer was new to the machine so they asked me to co-facilitate the training since I was the most familiar.

In the class were two guys from mainland China, Beijing I believe, one guy from South Korea, and one guy from Singapore, named Desmond. On a scale of 1-10 the guys from China spoke English on a scale of 6, the guy from Korea was a 4, and Desmond was a 10. The guy from Korea would take English classes before class and did the best he could. The Chinese guys seemed to understand it pretty well but were shy so they didn't talk much. Desmond was a 10 because he spoke fluent English with a super cute British accent. Singapore was once an English colony so English is their official language and he had gone to school in England. Singlish is their unofficial language, and I learned a lot of it from him (wah lau eh!) during our time together.

It was during this training session that I really realized how important my work was. One of my main tasks was to create documentation for repairing the equipment. I created hundreds of remove and replace, calibration, and similar documents for this piece of equipment. I took screenshots and photos and tried to make them as detailed as possible just to learn that they didn't follow them. During training, the instructor would encourage them to look up and then follow the directions. Since they *HAD* to, I watched them attempt to read the instructions and then gently ignore them.

What I observed was that they didn't have the skills or patience to read through paragraph after paragraph of instruction. They wanted bullet points, guidelines, and pictures. They also needed these instructions to be offline but not hard copies.

The class was 6 weeks long so after the first week we started to get to know each other better. We shared "American Sized" meals which they claimed was making them gain 10 kilos a week. We laughed at American TV and in general had a good time together. I am naturally curious, so I asked a lot of questions about their culture. At the time I didn't know a lot about China, so I had a ton of questions. Turns out, both of them were the year of the Dragon and so was I (1976).

The Year of the Dragon is a very special year (if I do say so myself). It is the token of authority, dignity, honor, success, and luck. Emperors entitled themselves exclusively as 'dragon' and many families wait to have their one child until the year of the Dragon. This is why I have worked with so many Dragons from both China and Taiwan.

It was funny because once we found out that we were almost all dragons I gained new respect from them. They never completely disregarded my instruction like the Japanese did but I could tell there was some reluctance. After the discovery that I was a Dragon my cool points went through the roof, and they started to treat me more like a friend than an outsider. To tell you the truth I didn't realize that they were treating me that way until they weren't.

Two weeks into the training, they were all feeling more comfortable with me, so they started asking me more questions (instead of me being Miss Nosy all the time). One day they asked if I was married, and I shook my head and said "No". Then they asked if I had kids.

So put this image in your head. We are in the clean room, fully suited up including gloves, suits, etc... I laugh and use my hand to say 0 kids. I put my thumb and forefinger together with the rest of my fingers to show 0. They start laughing and I ignore them. The next week they started calling me "Mama". I erroneously think it is because I did what I always have done and made myself the mom of the group. It was not until I asked Desmond that I realized what I had done.

Apparently, the Chinese count on one hand. In English, one is the pointer finger, then so on with five being the thumb and you continue to the next hand. Well in Chinese you only count with one hand, so one is the pointer finger and the number six, and a closed fist means 10. Apparently, when I tried to show the guys 0 they read it as 10 so I not only became Mama, I became Mama of 10 kids.

47

~

American Sized

The fun didn't stop there, every meal was a new experience. They tried Mexican, Thai, Hooters, Japanese, etc and they were always shocked by the "American Size" portions. I had had some experience internationally but there was always food just served differently so I didn't get it. Desmond especially loved the food and would talk about In and Out Burger, Chipotle, and other places he would find during his free time.

If he wasn't talking about American food he would talk about the food that I had to try when I visited Singapore. Most of his stories would include Chili Crab and Stingray. Desmond was the type of guy who couldn't just tell...you...a...story. HE....HAD...TO...TELL...YOU...A STORY ABOUT HOW AWESOME AND Phenomenal IT WAS and WHY YOU COULDN'T DO BETTER. Like me, he was expressive, talked with his hands, and tended to exaggerate which meant I instantly fell in love with him.

48

⌇

No Money No Honey

For such a small city/country Singapore has a strong Army/National Service. I tried looking it up for research, but I still don't understand it. Maybe my friend was in what we call the reserves. Who knows but, regardless, in early November 2005 I was sent to Singapore to cover for Desmond. He had to serve his country and I had to sit in a hotel room and cover him.

Most of my trips were last minute and I was the hero. I had to go in and save the day. Yes, me — female, white, mid to late 20s me!!

This case was different. There was no problem, and I didn't have my trusty CSE (Desmond) to take care of me and the customer. Don't get me wrong, Singapore is one of the safest places on the planet. I call it Asia for Dummies because it's clean and safe and they speak English. What can go wrong?

Actually... not much, to tell you the truth, and I really really tried to find trouble. Unfortunately, I was literally on call, and I felt like I was trapped in the hotel room. I didn't have an international cell phone and the team didn't have any way to contact me except through the hotel, so I didn't leave much during the day. Desmond had given me a ton of things to try but I was on a short leash.

I did manage to go out to the mall across the street and it was there that I discovered Chicken Rice. It's this amazingly simple dish that I fell in love with in Singapore and ate almost every day since it was only about $2 US. I also found a few local massage parlors because my back always hurts after long flights. That first week I played it pretty cool and explored locally.

Desmond had suggested I go to Sentosa Island, so I went there that weekend. Sentosa Island is a small tourist island outside of Singapore that used to host a fort during WW2. There are several ways to get there but I decided on the gondola lift. I love being in the air so this was a perfect way to get there until it started raining like crazy including thunder and lightning. It was scary because we were being tossed about in the wind and I was just sure we were going to be hit by lightning but of course, we didn't. As expected, on the other side of the ride was a gift shop, and since it was still raining I decided to check out the goods. I bought a few souvenirs and of course a couple of books. One of the books was called *No Money No Honey* and it was a book about the sex trade in Singapore which I had no idea about.

I was pretty naïve and just ignored the guys at work when they would talk about the "girlfriends" they had internationally. I would hear about Orchard Towers, but I didn't get it until I read this book. It really opened my eyes to little clues I had missed including at the massage parlor I had just gone to. I am glad I wasn't asked if I wanted a "Happy Ending" but I am pretty sure that is mostly a guy thing anyway. Apparently, a reporter interviewed several women and transgenders about their work. Needless to say, it ranged from simple legal massage parlors to down, dirty, and too X-rated for this book. There are some really interesting stories I like sharing, but those I only share in person.

Once the rain finally stopped I did manage to walk around the island. It's pretty small and I think I walked most of it. I watched the pink dolphin show, toured Fort Siloso, and hung out at the beach. It was a great escape from the hotel.

49

~

First Night Out

I don't know how I managed it, but it seems like every time I would travel to Asia it would be a holiday of some sort. One time in Japan, I had a Monday and Friday off due to the holidays. Having days off worked for me because the local engineers would take me sightseeing. Well turned out I was in Singapore during the Diwali Festival, and it has a huge Indian population, so I got to join in the festivities. A friend from my Motorola days, Michael, lived in Singapore and he met me one night to tour the city including Orchard Towers! We didn't start there of course because that is mostly for nightlife.

The first stop was a park that had amazing street food (Thai Satay) and then we went to get foot massages (reflexology) and then hit a couple of markets. One of the markets was in the Indian part of the city and it was like walking into a different country. The buildings, clothes, and language changed just by walking a couple of streets. There were decorations everywhere and you could feel the excitement in the air. As it got darker the streets got even livelier and the party started in the Hindi temple. The temple was surrounded by a wall and the gate had the most amazing decorations. It was dark but I still remember being in awe of it.

Inside the courtyard, hundreds of people were watching dancers dance on hot coals. I had seen traditional Indian dancing before at the Diwali

Festival in college, but they didn't do it on hot coals! Ok, Ok...not all of the dancers were on the coals but it certainly left an impression on me. We stayed and watched the dancing for a while and then headed to OT.

In all honesty, we were headed to Chinatown, dinner, and possibly a bar when we stumbled upon Orchard Towers, or OT as the locals call it. It wasn't as obvious as I would have thought, and we didn't even realize we were there at the time. The first four floors are home to famous bars aka brothels. I believe we went in because we saw signs for the bars. I bet you are thinking, wait a minute, I thought you were with a local? Yes and no, Michael had just moved there, and although he knew a few places he was also anxious to get out and explore. He was married with a young baby so didn't get out much.

So, the book had warned me about the prostitutes and brothels in Singapore, but I didn't realize I had just walked into the main area for this trade. The book was pretty generic about it and didn't mention OT by name. The OT isn't like Vegas or Amsterdam where there are naked women in the windows calling you in. There aren't any big glaring signs that say Girls Girls Girls (or Toy Boys). It looked like any shopping center but with bars in it.

The bar downstairs was like any other bar, and it wasn't really exciting so we checked out the bars on the other floors. Sure, there were half-dressed women everywhere, but it didn't look any different than the girls in the US hanging outside smoking, chatting, and waiting for friends. Again, call me naïve! It just wasn't obvious to me and they didn't talk to us.

As the night went on, and I finally figured out where we were, I was disappointed. Why didn't anyone hit on me or Michael? Not that I would have gone out with anyone, but it would have been nice to be asked. Did we look like a couple? Was it because Michael was Asian and not white? I will never know.

It certainly was an interesting experience. In one of the bars which also happened to have the best music, they had a stage where the "girls" would get up on the stage and show off their goods. They were mostly dressed, and they didn't strip, they just got up there and flaunted a little. What was weird was that most of them didn't even pretend to sell themselves. They didn't smile or flirt or entice the customers at all. They were boring and they all looked pretty much the same. Tiny Asian women with long black hair, short black dresses, and high heels. Weird...

A little disappointed that neither of us got hit on, we decided to leave and call it a night.

50

~

Going Going Back Back to... New York

As I mentioned in an earlier chapter, I ministered to over 30 teens when I lived in Arizona. Some of the teens just needed someone to listen to them but a few of them had serious issues including drugs, sex addiction, and cutting. One of the girls I was ministering to, Karla, was going through a divorce, well her parents were. She wasn't taking it so well and had started acting differently. She started wearing all black, Goth-like with very thick black makeup, she started smoking and she was cutting herself. At a retreat, she was even "spoken" to because she was behaving inappropriately.

The other core members tried too hard with her, they asked to pray with her and even tried talking with her parents. I would just listen. She and a couple of the other "troubled" teens would join my group and instead of forcing them to participate I just let them do their own thing. Don't get me wrong, I wouldn't let them act a fool, I just didn't force anything on them. I would check on them occasionally, ask their opinions on things, and listen. I could tell who was acting out, who was seriously confused, and who was just there because they had to be. I ministered to each in the way they needed me which, to the surprise of most people, is just to listen.

Karla and I grew closer, and we would often IM each other but mostly it was her talking about music. Since I didn't listen to the same music I couldn't relate to it, but I was there for her when she needed me. Although I didn't outwardly fuss over her or force her to do things, I was constantly praying for her, and some of the other teens who were dealing with major issues.

When I decided to move to CA, the most difficult thing was leaving my teens. Who would take care of them? Who would they have to help them? I was able to keep in touch with some of them and would see them at church when I visited my family. K and I kept in touch and, the Christmas after I moved to CA, I took her out to lunch. I drove to her house to pick her up and she came out wearing pink and green, not her usual black. She got in the car and told me she liked the music I was listening to, which was some hip-hop mix CD of my sisters. All very strange, who was this woman?

Karla was then in her senior year of high school and during lunch, she started describing her plans. She wanted to move to New York and go to fashion school. She had already started the process and she was determined to go. And go she did!

We continued to IM over the next year and when I was called to go to New York again right after Thanksgiving we agreed to meet. She had been telling me funny stories about her roommate, but I didn't really get it until right before I met up with them. I didn't watch much TV back then (and still don't) but her roommate Angela was Run's daughter. As in Run DMC and Run's House! I think I might have caught the show once or twice, but I really couldn't picture her in my head, and I certainly didn't think I would meet her but I did.

Karla and her boyfriend met me at the station, and we went to eat. We chatted about school and other stuff and then headed back to their dorm which was actually an older hotel. It was small but not any smaller than my dorm in college and they had an in-room bathroom. Turns out that night was the night Run's House normally aired so we all watched it together. It was a little weird watching a person on TV while they were in the room with you, but I got over it pretty fast. That was until her dad...as in Run...as in from Run DMC called! They laughed and chatted about the show and secretly inside I was dying and screaming...OMG!!! That was Run's voice I heard on the phone, I played it cool though and I don't think she noticed.

After the show, they walked me back to the train station and Angela called me out about my jeans. I was wearing Baby Phat jeans, which for those of you who don't know are designed by Kimora Lee, Russell Simmons' then-wife. Russell Simmons is Run's brother and the founder of Def Jam. She was like, "Did you wear those jeans because of me?" I replied, "No, these are the only jeans that will fit my big ass so all my jeans are Baby Phat." Which of course made everyone laugh.

51

~

Turning 30

Birthdays in our family were never really a big deal. When I was really young, my mom always worked nights, so she usually wasn't home to celebrate, and we never had extra money. To make it worse, my birthday is at the end of August so right before school starts, which means back-to-school supplies and clothes if we were really lucky. No extra money for gifts, cake, and parties. Mom did what she could and as I got older I started doing more for myself!

In 2006, I turned 30 and I decided I was going down in a big way! The best thing about turning 30 for me was that I had no regrets. I wasn't married nor had kids, but I didn't care. As I approached my birthday I looked back at my life and decided that I was exactly where I was supposed to be. This led me to make my 30th year - the best year ever! I booked a singles cruise and another trip to Europe.

I sent out an email to many of my friends for the cruise, but no one was able to go. Mostly, they were either pregnant or had young children so they couldn't leave. I ended up going on the cruise by myself and the singles cruise set me up with a roommate.

I connected with my roommate via email, and we ended up getting a hotel room together the night before the cruise. Her name was Shannon, and she was from DC. She was a beautiful black woman with two kids and was on vacation to get away from it all. We hit it off immediately; we were both loud, obnoxious, and ready to have fun!

On the day of the cruise, Shannon and I dropped our stuff in our room and went to the deck for the bon voyage party. We sat down and were instantly surrounded by men of all ages. They start asking questions and buying us drinks. One of the best conversations went like this:

Him - "Why are you on a singles cruise?"

Me - "I am turning 30 on Tuesday."

Him - "30? Well, there are 300 singles on this cruise, and it looks like it's about 50/50 so let's say there are 150 men. They can buy you 150 drinks for your birthday."

Me - "I can't drink 150 drinks."

Him - "100?"

Me - "No!"

Him - "50?"

Me - "No!"

Him - "Ok, how about 30 drinks? 30 for 30?"

Me - "OK, 30 drinks in 24 hours. I can probably handle that."

So, we end up clinking glasses and agreeing to that. Not that I care, I am always worried about money so I was hoping that I wouldn't spend a fortune on drinks.

52

❧

White Girl with the Big Ass

The cruise ends up being rerouted to different islands due to a possible hurricane. The day before my birthday was also our first stop. It was the Bahamas, which I had already been to, but this was my first time in Nassau. Shannon and I toured around Atlantis but then headed to the beach where we bought rum punch from a local vendor and laid out in the sun. We returned to the boat to find our room decorated with birthday decorations and full of presents. Apparently, my family had ordered a bunch of things to be delivered on my birthday. It was a nice surprise.

Shannon and I got ready for dinner by pre-partying of course. To save some money, we snuck in a lot of alcohol on board. Let me explain dinner on a cruise in case you have never been on one. Normally you get a choice of early or late dinner but since we were with a singles group, we automatically got the late dinner. The singles group was about 300 people on a cruise of 3000. We had our own section which was good because there weren't any young children.

We then headed to dinner where we had an assigned table but after the first night everyone kind of mixed and matched depending on who they hung out with that day. Shannon and I ended up at a round table for 10 people. The queen of the table, beside me, was an older woman named

Amy who had recently beat breast cancer. She was absolutely insane! She bought wine for the table and drinks for me to start celebrating.

A couple of the guys at the table bought me drinks as well and I think I had at least six drinks before dinner ended. After dinner, we decided to attend the "Adult Comedy Hour" at midnight (officially my birthday). We had an hour or so to kill so we headed to the casino to hang out. The word got around that my birthday was in a couple of hours, so people started offering me drinks. I was already pretty tipsy, so I turned most of them down but when they started offering kisses, I accepted. Even the ones, I wish I hadn't! There were a couple of feisty old guys I have a faint memory of. I didn't keep track of the # of kisses I accepted but I was keeping track of the number of drinks even though I didn't start officially counting until midnight.

At midnight, I was with one group of singles, and we sat in the lower seating area. I wasn't sure where Shannon was at this point, but I knew she was around somewhere. We got our seats and drink #1 was officially delivered. The comedian turned out to be a fine-ass black man with gorgeous lips. He came out on stage and welcomed everyone:

"How's everyone doing?"

We cheer!

"I heard there was a singles cruise on board."

We all start screaming!

He then says... "How do I get involved in that?"

I hear Shannon shouting from the balcony, "Just sign up, and come"

The comedian responds, "All I have to do to come is sign up? Sign me up!"

The audience roars with laughter, and I laugh and scream out, "But it's my birthday!" because of course no one should be the center of attention on my birthday but me.

Apparently, the comedian hears me, so he calls out, "Whose birthday is it?"

We all start screaming and he calls me on stage.

I went up, waved to the crowd, and smiled. The conversation then went like this:

"Where are you from?"

I answer, "California".

He says, "California? What are you doing on a cruise?"

I answer, "The water is cold there."

This gets a laugh from the audience.

He says, "So it's your birthday?"

I answer, "Yes!"

He asks, "So what are you doing for your birthday?"

I answer, "Collecting kisses and drinks."

He then says "Kisses? Well, here is your kiss."

He kisses me with his beautiful full lips and I can't help but think... "I am going to find your fine ass later"

He hugs me, and wishes me a Happy Birthday and then I start to walk off the stage. I get to the top of the stairs when he says, "That white girl has a big ass."

The crowd laughed, I stopped at the top of the stairs, did a little Beyoncé booty dance, and then took my seat. The crowd went wild and for the entire cruise I was either the white girl with the big ass or the birthday girl collecting kisses and drinks. I had 8 drinks before I went to bed that night. We enjoyed the comedy hour and then we hit the club!

53

~

Cruisin'

My actual birthday was a day at sea, so I woke up early, ate, found a spot on the deck, and then proceeded to go back to sleep. I had drunk way more than I had ever had in a short time, so I needed to continue to sleep it off. To be honest, I don't remember much about that day, but I do remember coming very close to my goal – 25 drinks in 24 hours!

I bet you are wondering if I met anyone on the singles cruise. No not really but I didn't expect to. There were a few guys my age, but I wasn't attracted to any of them, most of them were from the East Coast and I was there for fun! There was one guy who was super sexy but he ended up flirting with everyone, so I just went with it. There were a few love matches made and I even went to the wedding of one of the couples a few years later.

The cruise went to the Bahamas, Roatan (a small island off of Honduras), and St. Martin. I loved Roatan because it was still pretty undeveloped, and beautiful. A few of us singles ended up hanging out all day at a small bed and breakfast that served cheap drinks and great food! They had several hammocks that were perfect for hanging out in the shade and reading.

St. Martin (or Maarten on the Dutch side) was a super fun island that made some of the best rum I have ever tasted (I brought home four bottles). We spent some time shopping and then hanging out at a local touristy bar. Even in the middle of the day the DJ had us up and dancing on tables. At one point he is singing Hot Hot Hot and he picked me up and sings to me! Of course, since I love to be the center of attention I loved this!

I had a great time and I think the cruises are a great way to get a taste of new places. If you love a destination you can go back later! Best birthday ever!!!

54

∽

GOAL!!

Turning 30 Part 2 was a trip to Europe over Thanksgiving weekend. I went with a friend of a friend who needed a break from her husband and son. The few times we had hung out were fun and I had looked forward to traveling with her. I am a cheap traveler and I know how to look for deals but unbelievably she was even better! We decided we were going to go from Milan to Paris to Rome in a little over a week. I had been to Paris and Rome but with the church, so I was looking forward to going again. I had never been to Milan, so I was super excited about that part of the trip.

She was a soccer (football) fan, and she was scoping out Milan as a place to send her son for the summer to go to soccer camp. Milan is also known for its clubs and shopping so that is where we started.

We landed in Milan and after checking into our hotel we took a nap. We woke up and headed to the central part of the city for dinner. The restaurant we chose practically had you stacked on top of each other so you could hear everyone's conversations. Since most people were speaking Italian, our conversation must have stood out. People from the table next to us started talking to us. They were Middle Eastern or Indian, but it didn't matter to us. As we chatted with them we learned that one of the two had lost his wallet (or it was stolen). We felt bad for him, but we obviously didn't offer to help or pay for his dinner since he was with his friend. They told us they were engineers and were planning on visiting CA soon. I gave them my card and told them to call me when they were in town. Not a big deal, I like showing off CA and I wasn't remotely attracted to them. After dinner, they invited us to go with them to a nearby dance club. We were planning on going to the same place, so we joined them.

At first, the music was bumpin'! When we walked in a Beyoncé song was playing so I was happy with the choice. It cost 20 Euros to get in which did not make me happy, but it was Milan. At least they gave you a drink coupon so even though I had to pay cover at least I got a drink with it. My friend and I headed to the dance floor and started dancing. Sometime later, the guys came over and danced with us. As the song ends (or seems like it will), they ask if they can get us a drink. At first, I thought he was going to buy it for us but then I remembered the drink coupon and handed it over.

I asked for Vodka Lemon which should be vodka with lemonade or something close, but the guy brings me back basically a huge cup of vodka. At this time in my life, I was not a huge drinker (and it didn't taste good), so I just sipped on it. The music had changed so I sat down to rest my feet and drink. Unfortunately, the music I enjoyed wasn't what was on the playlist. From there, it was whistles, sirens, and that constant bump bump bump of house music. It wasn't too long before I got a headache and was ready to go so I grabbed my friend, and we took off. We briefly looked for the two guys, but we didn't see them, so we just left. What did it matter? We didn't promise them anything.

From there we party hopped down the street from one restaurant club to the next. We partied with Italians, the French, and even American military. We had a great time, drank a lot, danced a lot, and managed to find our way home by ourselves. It wasn't until the next morning that I realized that my American Express card was missing. Whether it was stolen, or I lost it is still a mystery, but the good thing is I was able to get my cash. While we were getting my cash we also checked in at home and wished our families a Happy Thanksgiving! It was weird because that was the second time in my life that I had missed Thanksgiving. The first was the year before when I couldn't make it because I had just bought my house and didn't have the money to visit, I missed my family, but I deserved this trip!

That night was the big soccer match. We spent the morning getting money and calling our families and the afternoon napping since we were still not used to the time change. We woke up and headed to the stadium.

One thing you should know about Europe (if you didn't get it from my previous chapters about walking in Germany) is that they really don't know how far they are walking! We asked the front desk clerk if we should take a taxi to the stadium, but the man said no, it's close. So, we walked...and walked...and walked... luckily we started early, so we got to the stadium before the game started. We waited in line (not really a line) for about ten minutes to find out we were in the wrong line. We then had to walk what seemed like a mile around the stadium to get to the correct ticket taker (the one who takes foreign-bought tickets). As we were waiting in yet another line (that is not a line) we heard the crowd in the stadium going wild as a goal was scored. We groan and can't wait to get in. It's obviously going to be a good match if a goal had already been scored in the first two minutes.

Well, needless to say, it wasn't a good match. That was the only goal scored for the entire match and we had missed it. We had great seats though and it was fun being in an Olympic-sized stadium but by the end, I was tired, hungry, and ready to go back to the hotel.

55

～

How I Met a Terrorist and Survived

We left the next morning for Paris. Luckily we left really early because we ended up at the wrong airport the first time. Who knew that there were two airports in Milan? Not us and our lack of Italian didn't help. We managed to catch another cab and catch our flight, but it probably cost us $100 extra.

We arrived in Paris and at our hotel too early to check in so we decided to take a walk along the Seine river and see where we would end up. One of the stops we had to take was an internet café where my friend checked her email. To tell you the truth, she did this a lot and it really annoyed me. I take vacations to get away from real life and I don't understand why people constantly feel like they have to "check in" all the time. In this case, it was even more annoying because we got an email from the guys we met in Milan.

The email starts by calling my friend a "Black Bitch". First of all, she was not black, African, or even Middle Eastern. She was Russian but she did have dark hair. Not sure where that came from but if that was a surprise the rest of the email was even more surprising. They start accusing us of using them, calling both of us names, and then threatening the US.

134 - *Craisiedaze*

They said all American women are whores etc... and they said that they were going to kill us all etc...

Wow! What do you do with that? Well, I Googled the FBI and decided to forward it to them. A week later we got a response from the FBI that these men were on the terrorist watch list and thanked us for helping them track them down. Yes, true story! I don't know what happened to them, but they scared me, and I hope they are rotting away somewhere dark and wet!

56

~

Montmartre

That little episode was just a tiny blip on our screen; we weren't going to let them hold us down. They were in Italy, and we were in Paris, a city of dreams, lights, love, etc.... We were on to our next adventure! Our hotel was super cute and typical of Paris, small with an elevator that could only carry one person and their luggage. It traveled so slowly that you could go up and down on foot in less time. The room was large, and the beds were small, but we didn't care because we were only there to sleep. We dropped off our stuff and headed out for a walking tour.

We met our tour guide at Moulin Rouge, and she proceeded to take us on a magical tour of the artistic part of Paris. We passed through places where Picasso and other painters got their inspiration, we shook hands with the statue of the man who walked through walls, we passed several windmills still in residence, and walked through the narrow pathways of the Montmartre Cemetery where some of the most famous Parisian artists are buried. The tour ended at the Sacre Coeur which watches over the city in perpetual adoration.

I say magical because it was. I could feel the power of the area as we explored its not-so-secret secrets. As we progressed through the tour it started to mist and it was easy to feel immersed in the culture and the art. Being the Catholic that I was at the time, I spent some time praying at

Sacre Coeur but afterward, I felt drawn to spend time in the area, so we had dinner in a small café. We warmed ourselves up with French Onion soup and ate enough French bread to feed a small nation. We then discovered it isn't easy to catch a cab while it's raining in Paris. We walked most of the way home and were soaked to the bone and freezing by the time we got back to the hotel. We promptly hung up our clothes, took warm showers, and passed out.

57

~

Real French Kisses

After our naps, we headed out to find some more adventure. What's funny is that, for a change, I didn't look like a foreigner; strangers approached us to ask for directions, in French. We answered in bad French, or maybe good but simple French saying I don't know (je ne sais pas). At one point we came across two extremely cute police officers and we asked them where we should go to hang out and we were told the Latin Quarter. We walked around for a bit and found a cute little bar where we ordered the appropriate Latin drink – a Mojito. Me being me, I flirted with everyone and finally got my first official French kiss, a kiss on each cheek like a native. It was awesome!

We hung out long enough for me to meet several people and collect data. I had just turned thirty and most of the people we met were in their 30s. We discussed this and determined it was because in Italy they married young and started families early. In France, they don't marry until their mid-30s and besides, they were more casual about sex. (Their words not mine)

This was proven by the Frenchman who proceeded to take me to the unisex bathroom to make out. This was my first time making out in a bathroom and should have been devastated when my friend broke in, but I wasn't.

58

~

Molested Much?

We only spent a few days in Paris, but it was fun and memorable. We found cheaper places to shop; where the clothes weren't in size negative. We spoke bad French but ate amazing food and flirted endlessly with the locals. No one made fun of us was rude, or ignored us. This was my second time in Paris, and I didn't experience any of the negatives that you hear about. We left Paris and headed to Rome in high spirits and ready for more adventure.

In Rome, we rented an apartment instead of a hotel room. It was cheaper and it was named the Daisy apartment which I, of course, loved! It was a three-bedroom apartment not far from everything and had a full kitchen and living room. I was a little disappointed in the washing machine because I couldn't figure out how to use it or it could have been that they were charging us more to use it. Who knows?

It was a cute place not far from a grocery store and other cute plazas and places to hang out. At one point we discovered a Gyro shop that is so much more. After my first visit, I start singing its praises. A popular song at the time was "I'm in love with a stripper" so I started singing "I'm in love with my sandwich" It really was one of the best sandwiches/gyros I had ever tasted, and it was worthy of my bad but gracious singing.

As I mentioned before Italians get married young which meant that most of the people out at the dance clubs were young people. Mostly around 24 which for the first couple of days was great. I was flattered that 24-year-old Italians were flirting with me, calling out "Ciao Bella", and making me feel like I was still in my 20s. Then it got old really fast. They were obnoxious, wouldn't take no for an answer, and were very very touchy-feely. On our next to last night, we were at a dance club and guy after guy was hugging and kissing all over me, putting hands down my shirt and pants and anywhere else they could manage. By the end of the night, I was exhausted from fighting them off and I had never felt so violated in my life. It never went too far but I was done with Italy! We had planned on going to an African/Reggae dance club on our last night, but I was mentally exhausted and didn't want to deal with another night of fighting off men. I know, I know, it sounds like a nice problem to have. Yeah, not really which is unfortunate because Italy is pretty awesome.

59

~

Give My Regards to Broadway

One of the great things about working in New York was the Broadway shows. I got good at finding the last-minute deals. I saw the Lion King, front row center and a bunch of us went to see Glengarry Glen Ross. We were late and had to watch standing up for the first half, but we enjoyed it.

I ended up back in New York at the beginning of 2007, right after New Year's. The tourists were gone, the streets were clean and quiet, and the hotels were super cheap. I stayed in a super cute boutique hotel in Times Square one weekend. It was easier than trying to catch the train back super late at night. I decided to go and try to see *Wicked*. They had a lottery system where they called your name for tickets. I added my name to both *Wicked* and the *25th Annual Putnam County Spelling Bee* which was in the theatre next door. I didn't win either but one lady who won the Spelling Bee lottery was single, so she invited me to join her for the matinee. Score!

I then went to the *Wicked* box office to see if they had any last-minute tickets. They apologized to me and said that they had exactly one left. I was like – well I am only one person, so it works for me. It was $100 for a center seat about 12 rows back – Perfect seats! So essentially I got two awesome shows for $100. I watched the Spelling Bee in the afternoon and then *Wicked* in the evening.

I enjoyed both of them, but *Wicked* did something to me. I left the show speechless. I got on the subway with other theatergoers, and I couldn't even join in on the conversation. I hadn't read the book (I know – shocking) so I went into the show clueless and left the show speechless. WOW! Talk about turning your whole belief system upside down!

I don't want to spoil it for you so I won't talk much about it but I will promote it! *Wicked* is a good example of why we shouldn't judge others. We only get a snapshot of a person; we don't know where they came from or what they went through to get where they are today.

60

~

TGI Fridays

Are you dizzy yet trying to figure out when and where I am and why? As you can tell between 2005 and 2010, I did a lot of traveling. I was mostly traveling for work and a lot of it was last minute. I was the fixer. When the stage went bad or someone needed coverage or training new employees, I was called to go.

At this point, I didn't even bother calling my mom to tell her I would be gone. I just said, if you haven't heard from me, it is probably because I am traveling. No news is good news. If I thought about it before I got on a plane, I would change my voicemail to inform whoever called that I was traveling. This was before smartphones were so popular. I had a BlackBerry at some point, but they didn't run on WIFI, and I didn't have an international plan. At some point, I bought a cheap unlocked phone to use with a prepaid SIM card, but sometimes it wasn't worth the trouble to get the SIM card. I was almost always being chaperoned by the locals or taking taxis (pre-Uber days).

After New York, I was soon flying back across the Pacific to our newest customer in Taiwan. I was covering for our Tech Support Engineer who was traveling for the Chinese New Year. They warned me that Taiwan would be more or less shut down for the week but semiconductor manufacturing stops for no man, woman, or holiday.

Traveling to Taiwan was different than Japan and Singapore. I wasn't trapped in my room, but I also didn't stay in the same hotel as my local team. In Japan, the CSEs and TSEs traveled every week to work from their hometowns. They stayed in the hotel and ate out every night. In Taiwan, the local team was local to that city, so they went home every night which meant I didn't have dinner companions. Hell, I barely had lunch companions. We would break for lunch and the team would go outside to smoke. I think they brought their lunch so they would just eat while they smoked.

Since they weren't with me, I had to "figure it out". Lunch was usually rice, some meat or fish, a salad, and a piece of fruit. Nothing too exotic or complicated except for the fruit. I didn't always know what the fruit was or how you ate it. Do you cut it? Bite into it? Peel it? It wasn't always obvious so I would have to wait until someone at a different table ate theirs.

In Hsinchu, Taiwan, I had two CSEs and a TSE that covered Hsinchu and Kaohsiung. All men but also all dragons. Unlike in Japan, there were women engineers and technicians here; they just weren't on my team. I never had an issue with my team following my leadership, but they also weren't very social, so I had to fend for myself for dinner.

My hotel had a TGIFridays on the street level and a shopping center with a food court at the basement level. It was fun exploring the shopping center during Chinese New Year. It was the Year of the Pig. Not the major year, but "Pigs" are meant to bring joy, happiness, and innocence into life, and you could feel the joy radiating from the decorations, displays, and altars. Some displays even had live baby piglets in them. It was cute seeing them snort, squeal, and squiggle around.

Whenever I eat alone, I bring a book to keep me company and to entertain myself. Eating at the food court was the cheapest option but it was always very bright, cold, and impersonal there so when I wanted company, I would go to TGIFridays. I usually sat at the bar when I was alone, read my book, and chatted with the people around me if they were the chatty type.

I hit the chatty jackpot as soon as I sat down at the TGIFridays bar and met the abominable and adorable Lily. There weren't too many people in the restaurant, so Lily was practicing her bartending cocktail-throwing skills. She was juggling/tossing two cocktail shakers, chatting with a waitress while bouncing around the bar, and had a smile for everyone. I loved her immediately. As soon as I sat down, she gave her shakers a final toss, sat them down and we started chatting.

Lily was in her mid-20s, had gone to school for restaurant management, had a fiancé, and was practicing for a cocktail-throwing tournament. She said, "Like the Tom Cruise movie - Cocktail." Previously she had been using practice shakers, the tops and bottoms were taped together, but she showed me a couple of her signature moves while making me her signature drink. She was a lot of fun and we got to know each other well while I was there for those two weeks. In between customers, she would ask lots of questions about life in California and America, about my family, why I don't have a boyfriend and more.

I don't normally like to go to American places when I am traveling to foreign countries, I prefer to eat local food but I when I was in Hsinchu, Taiwan I went to TGIFridays to see Lily. We kept in touch via email for a long time (pre-Facebook days) and I was even invited to her wedding which was to be in Singapore. I tried hard to go, I even asked Desmond to break something, so I had an excuse, but it didn't work out for some reason. She sent me pictures instead and I was sad to have missed it. It would have been amazing to see a wedding in Singapore, I often wonder if it would have been similar to "Crazy Rich Asians"?

61

~

Flying 36 hours for 24 hours in Singapore

While I didn't make it to Singapore for the wedding, I did have to fly to Singapore unexpectedly. Why were most of my trips last minute? Why was this trip different? Great questions! My first trip to Singapore wasn't unexpected since I was covering for Desmond, but my second trip was an extreme example of last minute. I was a "New Product Engineer" remember? This meant all our systems were still in the Beta stage. The customer understood that they were still in the Beta stage when they purchased them. They also understood that things could break but we fully supported them 24-7. This meant a lot of late-night phone calls, conference calls with the design team, and last-minute trips. Usually, I was able to fly out late that evening or early the next day. I had time to pack my bag and then head to the airport.

I lived in San Jose but usually flew out of SFO since it had many nonstop flights to Asia. Flying to Japan and Taiwan was easy, there were several nonstop flights a day. At that time Singapore was more difficult. It was further away and even flying Singapore Airlines; I would have to stop in Hong Kong. This trip to Singapore was because we had an important demonstration (demo) for the customer and one of the parts was malfunctioning. Normally, we have a stock of parts locally and we did have this part in stock, but the replacement part didn't work either, so someone needed to deliver the part to the customer ASAP.

(This is where if I was chatting with you on the couch, I would get distracted and tell you all about my annoying coworker who fell in love with a girl in Taiwan and was useless after that, but I am hoping to get this book out before I die so I will not digress.)

I was the only one who could go. I needed to hand-carry this part to Singapore in time for Desmond to install it and the Application Engineer can set it up in time for the all-important demo. Piece of cake!

NOT! Everyone was freaking out. The designers were testing and verifying the part I was going to take was working correctly, the manufacturing team was anxiously waiting for the testing to be done so they could remove the part from the machine they were building, the logistics team was trying to get the paperwork ready for me to bring the part into the country and I was trying to find a flight. The flight I would normally take was sold out so the best I could find was San Jose to Los Angeles to Hong Kong to Singapore. I booked it, went to the logistics building to get the paperwork, and then headed to manufacturing to pick up the part. I then headed home, packed just an overnight backpack, and headed to the airport.

So far so good but unfortunately, they wouldn't let me take the part on board with me. I had to check it which made me extremely nervous. How do I know that it won't get damaged? How can I ensure it won't get lost? They absolutely refused to let me bring it on board. In hindsight, maybe I should have purchased a seat for it. For perspective, this part was about 40 lbs, the size of a 2007 desktop computer, and worth $200,000. It was essentially our machine's CPU. There was a lot at stake but there wasn't much I could do.

Off to LA, I went, but I had a long layover. Which was not horrible assuming the plane wasn't delayed. I settled in at an airport bar to have dinner and read. At some point, while I was at the bar a bunch of young men joined me. They were heading somewhere for a bachelor party, but their flight was delayed so they started the celebration at the airport. They were very obviously well off, and they were very generous. They bought me several drinks and we had a great time talking about who knows what. Eventually, we head off to our respective flights all pretty tipsy. My flight was at midnight so I was glad to be tipsy, it would help me sleep on the plane. Unfortunately, when I got to the gate, they announced that they were delayed, and I would miss my connection.

UGH! I had to let Desmond know which meant taking out my computer, logging into WIFI, and then emailing him the details. I think this experience was what justified getting a BlackBerry.

We finally boarded and I was half asleep when I heard that we needed to make an emergency stop in Alaska. Alaska??? Why were we even close to Alaska? Shouldn't we just zip across the ocean to Hong Kong? Why go North to go South? At this point, I was trapped, and I had no method of communicating with anyone, so I went back to sleep and woke up in Alaska.

Not sure how long we were there but we didn't have to deplane so it must not have been too bad of an emergency. The next time I woke up we were in Hong Kong. I had been traveling for almost 24 hours at this point and all I wanted to do was brush my teeth and take a shower. Some of the major airports will have lounges with showers that you can be a member of or pay to get in.

That had to wait though until I figured out how I was getting to Singapore now that I missed my connecting flight. After waiting in line forever I finally got my flights taken care of, yes you read that correctly, flights. I had to go from Hong Kong to Taiwan to Singapore.

I was so pissed off and disoriented (and probably hungover) that it took me forever to find a lounge that I could use. I brushed my teeth but decided against a shower since I only had a day's worth of clothes and limited time. I then got my computer out, logged into WIFI, and emailed Desmond my new arrival time. He was planning on meeting me at the airport and then taking me to the hotel but since I was so late, he would meet me at the airport, grab the part and I would take a taxi to the hotel where I would sleep for 4 hours and then fly home.

After traveling for 36 hours through five airports I finally arrived in

Singapore. I headed to the baggage claim area and started praying. Please let the part be there, please let it be undamaged, please let Desmond be there. After what seemed like forever I saw the part, I picked it up and headed towards the exit where a guard stopped me and asked what I had in the box. This was where being in an English-speaking company was actually a negative. If I had been in Japan, I could have played dumb and tried to talk my way out of it, but I can't do that there.

He pointed me toward what I think was a Customs room. I wasn't too nervous, I wanted to skip Customs so I could get the part to Desmond faster, but I wasn't that lucky. I went to Customs, dug the paperwork out of my bag, and handed it to the agent. The agent promptly asks for more paperwork. More? I didn't have more. I was close to tears, I was tired and hungry, and I needed to pee and brush my teeth. The guy must have seen the look on my face because he asked what it was. I said something about a part for work and when he asked how much it was worth. I lied and said $10,000. He made me pay some tax which I tried to put on my Corporate Travel card, but it was denied! He tried again but it was denied. My corporate "travel" card!

I finally used my debit card (I was avoiding personal credit cards at this point) and ran to meet Desmond. He met me as soon as I exited the terminal, grabbed the part, and ran off to deliver it, 12 hours or more after my original arrival time. I hit the restroom and grabbed a taxi to the hotel. I attempted to use my travel card again, but it was denied so I used my debit card again. Why do I mention this several times? It was like the 30th or something and I had scheduled my mortgage payment to be paid on the 1st and it was now about to bounce. On my way to my room, I had "boing" and "bounce, bounce, bounce" running through my head. I got to my room, ran to the desk, took out my computer, and attempted to log into WIFI. No signal. No ethernet cable outlets but I didn't bring a cable anyway. UGH!

I walked around the room trying to find a signal, but I couldn't find one. I stepped out into the hallway, and I got one. I logged into my account and transferred some money to cover my mortgage. I took a deep breath, returned to my room, found my toothbrush, and brushed my teeth. I was about to take a shower when I remembered the stupid travel card. I called the 800 number from the hotel phone knowing it would be a gazillion dollars but fuck it. My company owed me big time after all this shit. When someone finally answered they told me I was supposed to inform them of when and where I was traveling. Are you fucking kidding me? This is a "travel" card. It says it in the name, I bought my flights with it, and I never had issues before so why now? They blamed it on some policy or another and asked if I wanted to turn it back on. Uh.....YES!!

I hung up and was headed to the shower when my phone rang. It was Desmond, the application engineer was nervous and wanted me to stay another day - just in case. Fine! I took a shower, threw my travel clothes in a laundry bag to be washed, and passed out for what seemed forever. I woke up to the phone ringing. They wanted to thank me with dinner. Damn right, you did!

62

Chili Crab, Stingray, and Chijmes

This was my third or fourth trip to Singapore. I was traveling so much and so often some of the details are running together. My second time there I got to work and hang out with Desmond. He took me to eat Chili Crab as soon as he picked me up from the airport. It was messy but absolutely delicious. I love crab in general, but this was a soft-shelled crab covered in chili sauce.

I don't remember why I was in Singapore at that time, but I remember him taking Matt and me to the "Long Bar" to have a Singapore Sling and then walking to Chijmes for dinner. Chijmes was originally a Catholic Convent but now housed bars and restaurants. It is pretty expensive, so when I went there with Desmond, we just went to a dive bar there to hang out.

This time the application team was paying for dinner, so Chijmes it was. I don't remember the name of the restaurant but when I saw Stingray on the menu, I didn't hesitate to order it based on Desmond's constant chatter about it. Boy oh boy was he correct! Another delicious dish. It reminded me a lot of scallops, it had the same texture, was prepared like scallops, and was even cut in circles. When I mentioned that to the table, I learned that sometimes stingray was used instead of scallops. Interesting indeed!

The demo team I met for this trip was interesting. They were composed of an application engineer, a sales engineer, and someone else I can't remember. All white males. I worked with the application engineer before, but I didn't like him. He was a short overweight British guy with red hair, freckles everywhere, and bad teeth. He was married to a Japanese woman he met while working there and was constantly in a bad mood. In the US, we didn't hang out unless it was a team meeting because I didn't like being around moody negative people but when traveling, you make do. Especially when they were paying for it.

Hanging out with all men internationally always ends up the same way. Dinner, after-dinner drinks, bar, girls. At this point, I am just one of the guys and they don't mess with me. Occasionally, though, they get a little weird. This night was a good example. The dinner conversation was boring, they mostly talked about the day, the customer, and other boring stuff, so at some point I excused myself to go to the bathroom. We were done with dinner and just chatting over drinks, so I left the restaurant to search for the bathroom. After the bathroom, I passed the bar that I had been to with Desmond on a previous trip, so I went in. I can't remember why I was in there for longer than a minute but the next thing I knew one of the guys came in all out of breath and worried about me. I guess when I didn't come back right away, they went looking for me. Weird.

The rest of the night went as expected. We went back to that bar to have a drink then headed to the OT. This time it was a different experience since I was with three white guys. I still didn't get propositioned or hit on, but the guys certainly did. It was a little disappointing seeing my married coworkers flirt and make out with other women but when in Singapore...

63

Man Jose

It was hard to have a relationship during this time and I didn't. I was dating and even kind of considering marriage, but I was never in town long enough. San Jose is often called Man Jose due to all the technology jobs there which were still mostly filled by men.

Sounds perfect right? Wrong!

Let's break it down for those of you who haven't been there. Silicon Valley is huge, and traffic is terrible. I remember thinking, if you can't get to my house in 20 minutes or less, I am not interested. It is also very expensive which means you need to have a high-paying tech job or multiple jobs.

Also, have you met an engineer? Most are introverted, shy, and more interested in their computer/gaming system than girls. This means that most of the men I dated were not in the tech industry. Between my job that took me away unexpectedly and them working multiple jobs - I stayed single.

I had my good times and bad times with this. Like anyone in their early 30s, I wanted to be in a relationship. I didn't date the last couple of years in Arizona because I wanted to make sure I was OK. I wanted to be a better person, I had to love myself before someone could love me.

Through counseling, ACA, and Life Teen I was able to shed some of those masks and learn to love myself.

I was excited to start over in San Jose, a new place, a new me. I have now relocated several times and I love starting over. You can reinvent yourself. Leave the old negative stuff in the past and literally move on. My first weekend in San Jose I went club hopping by myself!

I did all the things - met guys in bars, church, and grocery shopping, I tried online dating, craigslist, friends of friends, and even men I worked with but none of them were keepers or if they were, they didn't think I was.

I was also a little turned off by my coworker's behavior. Knowing that everyone had side pieces in different countries was disconcerting. When I was open to dating and marriage, I remember telling myself I wouldn't be with anyone who traveled.

64

Creating Something New

In 2007, I changed jobs. I was hired by Chris who I respected. He and I communicated well, he knew how to work with me (timelines and words of affirmation) and he went to bat for me to get paid the same as my male colleagues. He was prepping for me to take over his job but then he was laid off. Instead of promoting me though they promoted my teammate because he had more experience aka, he was an older white man. He wasn't so bad, and I still wanted to travel so I only complained a little. Not too long into the job he quits and takes another job. It was a good move for him and his family, but it wasn't great for me.

The guy that they replaced him with did not like me at all. He was an application engineer (software not hardware), had never done what I did, and didn't trust me. I was taller than him, louder than him, and had more personality. We butted heads immediately and I was so miserable that I ended up changing departments and eventually companies.

Remember my friend and coworker Corey? He went to work for Palm, as in the Palm Pilot and the original smartphone the Palm Treo. He loved what he did and anytime there was an opening he would tell me to apply. I interviewed for one position which I didn't get but when a better position opened, they offered that one to me instead. Again, as a New Product Engineer, I was to help bring new phones to market. I would have early prototypes which I would help test by using them and I would provide feedback to the design team. I also helped write training and troubleshooting materials for the website and the call centers. My original product was their last smartphone with the Windows Operating System. I traveled domestically for this launch to support the call centers in Dallas and Denver.

Unfortunately, this phone didn't do so well in sales because the iPhone was launched around the same time. BlackBerry still owned the market when I started with Palm but when the iPhone came out, it changed the game. Palm was already developing a new phone and new OS, but it was still in the alpha stage.

Once the WebOS and PalmPre were in the beta stage, it was all hands on deck. We created something brand new, so we need to change our brand, our website, and our support methods. It was an exciting time to be at Palm. Our stock split, we were busy, and we were having fun creating a whole new world.

By this time, I was in grad school, it was a two-year program that met twice a week and kept me reading and writing the other nights of the week and on weekends. I dated less to concentrate on school and had to step back from Life Teen. My free time was breaks between quarters.

In early 2009, we were preparing to launch the Pre. Several of my colleagues had been to our call centers in India and the Philippines (PI) but I hadn't gone yet. I was still traveling but for fun. I had gone on a couple more cruises and a few trips to Mexico and Hawaii. I even attended another WYD in Australia in 2008 where we traveled to both New Zealand and Sydney.

I was busy but I have always thrived in busy chaotic environments. I don't remember why but for some reason my boss couldn't travel to the Philippines as scheduled so he asked if I could go to support the training classes. This made sense since I created most of the materials. I was super excited to go because I love the Filipino culture and I had yearned to travel there. The only issue was timing.

65

Around the World in 30 Days

I had planned on going back to Hawaii for spring break, but I also had a trip to Rolla planned for a Chi O anniversary event a couple of weeks later. This trip meant I would go from Hawaii to PI to St Louis to Rolla in less than 30 days. It was going to be one hell of a trip and it certainly was. Since the trip was no longer than a week, I had to work it out with my professor. Technically you couldn't miss any classes since we were on a fast-tracked schedule but the class, I was going to miss was a test, so he agreed to let me take it from PI.

My cousin William is a Marine and was stationed in Hawaii at this time. I think this was my third trip to visit him. Hawaiian Airlines had a direct flight from San Jose to Oahu and great deals. He was still new so he couldn't spend much time with me, but I was OK with that. All I needed was a beach and a book. Since this was a long trip, I brought all six of the Sookie Stackhouse books with me. (IFKYK)

This trip to Hawaii was certainly one for the her-story books. Since my cousin was busy, I did my normal thing of meeting strangers and getting into trouble. Normally the trouble I get into involves strange men and fun but this time it didn't end up as I had hoped. There was a fun strange man involved. He was the lunchtime bartender at the restaurant I went to on the beach. I did my normal eat/read at the bar and we got to talking. He invited me out to drink at a local spot later which was a much better experience than a touristy restaurant. At some point, my cousin joined us, and we all drank way too much but had a lot of fun talking shit and hanging out with other beach bums.

That doesn't sound so bad, does it? Well, the night was just getting started. While walking home a few locals started talking shit to us and of course, my drunk ass said something like, "You better watch out, my cousin is a Marine" and then all hell broke loose.

The girl in the group slapped me. WTF? The last person who slapped me was my mother when I was 14 and when I was talking back to her. I was so shocked I didn't know what to do. I stood there but they all took off running. My cousin was pissed, but he walked me back to the hotel and then took off after them. He had been a boxer in high school so I knew he could fight but I was still scared. I sat on the steps waiting for him to get back. I don't remember how long he was gone but he came back with a black eye. I knew he would get in trouble at work, but it wasn't as bad as we thought once he explained he was defending me.

Wish I could say that trip got better but it didn't. A couple of days later after a day at the beach and then drinking a dangerous fishbowl drink with my cousin, we were skipping (yes literally skipping) back to the hotel when I tripped on a crack in the sidewalk and fell flat on my face. I chipped my tooth (really the cap just fell off) and I thought I broke my face/nose. My cousin got me to my room and threw me in the shower to wash all the blood off. I woke up the next morning with a sore cheek, black eyes, and a busted lip. How embarrassing!

I took a cab to the urgent care to get checked out and luckily besides my tooth, nothing was broken. At this point, I decided to chill out on the Spring Break shenanigans. I was acting like a 22-year-old, not a 32-year-old who had to go to PI in three days. My face was all black and blue, so I didn't feel like being social. Instead, I hung out by the pool and proceeded to get sunburned.

Boy, I really screwed up this trip! I was now black, blue, and red! How was I going to be the professional looking so horrible? Well, I decided to have a great story and rest for the next two days. I still hung out by the pool, but I hid from the sun in a tent and slathered on the sunblock. Regardless, I was pretty miserable by the time I was on my way to PI.

66

Mabuhay

I looked so bad that my neighbor on the plane gave me some stem cell stuff to put on my face. At this point, I didn't think it would make it any worse, so I did. I am not sure how much it helped but I eventually healed, and I only have a tiny scar to remind me of my foolishness. That and regular Facebook posts from my cousin.

Once I got to Cebu, I was still sunburned, but my black eyes were now greenish-yellow. I looked sickly but I made up a fun surfing story that I used to explain the bruises and scabs. I was met in Cebu by a driver who took me to the hotel/mall where I experienced something I had never experienced before, and I was shocked. The security was insane. To get to the hotel, we went through a gate where a guard first had to check the underside of the van with a mirror, then had the driver turn on the interior light to show me. Once we got to the hotel, I had to walk through a metal detector and my bags go through an x-ray machine like in the airport. Very weird! Was there a lot of terrorism in the Philippines that I don't know about? What danger was I facing? Who were we afraid of?

I didn't have time to dwell on it because I was scheduled to meet the team for dinner. I went up to my room, brushed my teeth, showered, and changed. In the lobby, I met Marcella, whom I knew from the San Jose office. She was one of the Call Center Operations Managers. She flew between our call centers in the Philippines, India, and Argentina often. When not in San Jose, she spent most of her time in India, but like the rest of us, we went where we were needed. She was a little older than I was but had great friendly energy. I also met Mark, who was the training manager and worked remotely. I think I had only met him a few times in the office when he visited before this trip. In general, I liked everyone I worked with at Palm, we were like a start-up at the time. Everyone is working hard to accomplish something great. I was excited to be in Cebu with this team.

I arrived Sunday night, so we had dinner to discuss the plans for the week. I was there to support Mark who did the actual training. I was the Subject Matter Expert (SME) who could answer the more technical questions. I think we were a month or two prelaunch. We were there to train the call center operators on the new phone and OS so they would be ready for Go-Live.

Palm had found that people were confused about how to use and set up smartphones. They would return the phone if it wasn't super easy to set up, so to avoid returns, they created what they called the "Butler" service. They listed the call center support number on the phone and would help assist users in setting it up. We had a US voice call center in Cebu City, Philippines, a US chat center in Hyderabad, India, and a European voice and chat center in Buenos Aries, Argentina.

The PI and India centers supported US customers in US time zones which meant they worked the night shift which meant so did I when I was there. It helped a little with the jet lag, but my body didn't enjoy being awake when it was dark outside and it was hard to fall asleep during the day. My schedule was this: Wake up and have dinner for breakfast since it was about 6 pm, head into the office around 8 pm, and break for lunch around midnight. Then work till about 6 am and return to the hotel where I would have breakfast for dinner. I would then sit by the pool for a couple of hours before going to bed between 10-12.

I loved my time working at the call center. The level-one support teams we were training were all brand-new employees, so they were eager to learn and get started. Most of them were engineers but we did have a few nurses and other degrees. To work in our call centers, they had to have a degree and speak English fluently. At the time we were right in the middle of the pay scale in comparison to other centers. We paid better than most but not the best which reflected in the level of English. If you get a call center operator who you can't understand, they are probably on the lower end of the pay scale. If you think you are speaking to a US citizen, you might be because there are still several US call centers, but you might be talking to someone in the Philippines who works for a company that pays very well.

While I was there, I also worked with our Level 2 and Level 3 support teams. They had been with us for a while and were the local experts. If they ran into issues they couldn't resolve, they reported the bug and worked with my team to get it resolved. I had heard these voices at least once a week for almost two years, so it was nice to finally meet them in person and get a face with the name. They were all men, but the actual call center manager was a young woman named Irene. She had a law degree but there weren't many jobs in that field, so she went into operations management.

Irene was an incredibly intelligent no-nonsense woman in the office, but we got a chance to hang out with her out of the office. We were there for two weeks so we had a weekend off. This was my first time in Cebu, so she decided to show it off a little. Saturday, she took the three of us to the Shangri-La for a day trip. We sat by the beach, swam in the warm ocean, and had a marvelous seafood dinner. It was Easter weekend, so she took Marcella and me to mass and touring around the city on Sunday followed by more incredible food.

I am not quite a foody, but I am close, and I absolutely love Filipino food. I had a good friend in middle school who was Filipino, and I spent a lot of time at her house. I didn't know all the names of the dishes then but once I moved to San Jose, I got very familiar with them. Between my roommate Pauline and the Mamas at my church, I could identify most Filipino food if not by sight but by taste. The Mamas even taught me how to roll lumpia and make Adobo and Pancit for the many fundraisers we had. I don't make my own lumpia, but I still make Adobo and Pancit regularly.

At this time, Cebu City was a fairly new call center city. Most had been and still are in Manila, but many companies branched out to Cebu which was cheaper and less crowded. Today there is a whole eco-system for supporting workers who work at night. More restaurants are open later and other services are offered at the time when others are sleeping. Back then though, it was still pretty new so there weren't many restaurants. We could choose between McDonald's and Jollibee, which is famous for its fried chicken. Most of my colleagues went with that. A couple of guys ate at McDonald's every day. They were very picky about food.

Not me! I tried anything and everything, from the hole-in-the-wall shack with food in pots to the tin roof-covered outdoor restaurant that served BBQ. I tried it all and never got tired of it or got sick. It was definitely an experience I wish I would have documented more. I was Anthony Bourdain before there was an Anthony Bourdain. OK, my timing is probably off, but you get the idea.

67

∽

80/20 rule

After an amazing but exhausting trip to the Philippines, I flew to St. Louis. I stayed with my sorority little – little – little sis, Kristen. She had been a freshman when I was a senior, but we had hit it off immediately. She was from Kansas City as well and her mom and I even have the same birthday. Kristen and I kept in touch and every time I was in St. Louis, I tried to stay with her. She and her husband were both rum drinkers, so I brought them some amazing (and super cheap) rum from the Philippines. They had recently bought a new house and the patio had been installed so I sat outside with them and chatted over glasses of Filipino rum. When I travel, I try to connect with friends. When traveling to Dallas and Denver I met up with other sorority sisters, Ginger and Sarah.

Early the next morning I went down to Rolla, MO. Chi O was having another one of those 5-year anniversary things. JL, my college roommate, and still good friend was now living there so it was a good excuse to catch up with her. She and her husband had also just bought a new house, so I stayed with them for the weekend. Once again, we sat on their porch and drank rum but JL's husband, being the tech geek he was, peppered me with a bunch of questions about the new PalmPre smartphone. He wanted one but knew the FBI wouldn't let him use it since it had a camera. Oh, how things would change...

The night of the anniversary dinner was busy. Dinner, speeches, and then drinks at a bar somewhere to catch up with old friends and meet new ones. A conversation at the bar changed my life.

"Sorry ladies, I am still jet-lagged after my trip to the Philippines," I said after yawning for the gazillionth time.

After having heard of some of my Hawaiian and Filipino adventures one of them said, "Wow, I wish I had your life. You can go anywhere you want, fuck whoever you want, and do anything you want."

"Maybe I want your life. You are the CEO of your own company that is very successful, you are married and have two beautiful kids," I countered.

"Yeah, I am happy about 75% of the time," she countered back.

I thought about that and said "Girl, you are right. I am happy 90% of the time. Why would I trade my 90% for your 75%?"

That night my 80/20 Happiness rule was established. I decided that I was happy and that happiness was a choice. I choose to be happy. I thought that 90% might be too hard to maintain though so I decided that I would be happy 80% of the time. I gave myself 20% of my time to be sad, lonely, heartbroken, etc. but if it got to be more than 20% then I would need to make a change. Only I can make myself happy and I am worth it.

68

~

Almost Dying in Two Countries Part 1

Soon after I returned to the US, I was asked to go to the India chat center to support training there as well. I was a little surprised by this request but still excited to meet my Level 3 team there and learn more about India. Over the years I have had several close Indian friends, and I am sure you won't be surprised to hear that I loved the food. Unlike the Philippines though, my coworkers didn't have as many stories about India.

While booking my flights I learned that I had a long layover in Dubai on the flight back and I could stay a night for no extra flight fee. Yes, please! I had heard some pretty exciting things about Dubai including that they were building the tallest building in the world, they had created man-made islands that looked like a Palm tree, and they had indoor skiing. It sounded incredible!

First, I had to get the work done in India. Unfortunately, I didn't do a good job of researching where I was going. I made the mistake of thinking that all of India was like Bollywood movies. Hell, I had watched Slumdog Millionaire. I thought I was prepared; I was not.

Our center was in Hyderabad, India, which I had learned before the trip was the Silicon Valley/tech center of India. (This surprised me - I thought it was Bangalore) I assumed it would be like Cebu, so I didn't think to research it more.

When I arrived in Hyderabad, it looked like any other airport until I exited the building. It was evening so very dark but there were hundreds of people waiting outside. It was chaotic, noisy, and confusing. Where was my driver? Did they forget me? This is always the most nerve-racking part of traveling - connecting with the driver. I finally find a sign with my name, and I must push and squeeze through the crowd of mostly men to get to the driver. There weren't too many women who were waiting but those who were there were the ones that surprised me. They were covered from head to toe in black burqas. I was expecting bright colors, scarves, Saris, and Salwar Kameez (yes, I had to google it), not burqas. Had I somehow ended up in Saudi Arabia or Iraq?

I am still surprised to this day by how shocked I was to see this. I feel like I am the most open-minded, coolest person in the world. I love culture and diversity so why was I so shocked? In hindsight, I blame the media. They are ones who associated burqas to danger, they are the ones who blast pictures of women in burqas holding machine guns.

My driver didn't help with my shock or nervousness. He took my bag and quickly walked away. I followed him until he stopped at a random street and told me to wait. He left to get the van with me waiting on the street with my carry-on roller bag and backpack. WTF dude? I could have gone with you. I felt like a target waiting on that street. It took forever but, eventually, he pulled up and I got into the van. We then take off for the hotel.

The drive seems to take forever. It was dark and at first, all I could see were empty fields but after a while, we entered the edge of the city. I remember seeing lots of construction in progress but also lots of abandoned and collapsed buildings. A new well-kept building would be next to a building that was ½ ruble. The city had a yellow glow from streetlights. It was very creepy, and it got creepier when the driver stopped in the middle of nowhere for seemingly no reason. He didn't say anything, just got out and didn't come back for 15 minutes. Again, I felt like a target. Luckily, he did return. I don't know what he did, and I didn't ask. I just wanted to get to the hotel and brush my teeth (see a trend). I was staying at "Taj" something or other which was absolutely majestic and beautiful but like the hotel in Cebu, we had to go through all the security procedures. Check the van for bombs and go through metal detectors and x-ray machines.

Also like the Philippines, the Indian team worked US hours so I followed the same schedule there. A different driver, a lot more talkative and friendly, picked me up the next night for work. Since it was dark, I couldn't see much except for the outlines of buildings. The call center was a nice building in what looked like the middle of nothing. Fields and mounds of dirt surrounded the place. Vans like mine were moving in and out of the area dropping off riders.

Once I arrived on our floor, my anxiety left me. My level 3's greeted me along with the center manager. He was around my age and had worked in semiconductors too, so we had a lot in common. They were all excited to show me around and explain the setup. Since it was a chat center it wasn't as "buzzy" as the Cebu center was but there were still people chatting with each other, laughing, and moving around.

What I did notice was that there were only 2 women. I didn't get a chance to ask about this till my second trip, but I learned that they recruited women, but they had a low retention rate. Women usually only lasted about two months. The two women that were there when I was, were long-timers. They had been there for a while and were rebellious. One night, I watched one woman get off a motorcycle, and walk into the building and by the time we reached our floor, she had her burqa off. I was too nervous to ask her about it but it felt like she had made the statement, so I didn't need to ask. Years later I would read "Reading Lolita in Tehran" and discuss the book with an Iroquoian woman friend of mine, but I would think of this woman often and all the questions I had wanted to ask.

Was it fear or respect that held me back? Probably both. I was afraid. I was afraid to offend her, I was afraid to sound ignorant, uneducated, racist, and I was afraid of what I would hear. Talking to my immigrant friends who have lived in the US most of their lives is not the same. Most of them haven't lived through it, they escaped young and adapted to American life.

This first time in the India office I was very nervous and cautious. I didn't have anyone with me from the US and I hadn't been warned about what to expect. I was given a space to work, and I would wander around occasionally to work with the teams that needed me to help respond to chats. One day I wore slightly cropped pants that rose up when I sat down. I have a tattoo of a cross on my right ankle and that became the talk of the center for the whole night.

Most nights we would lose power. There were generators for the chat team's computers but suddenly being thrown into the dark was alarming. We would lose lights and air conditioning. We could walk around by the glow of the computer screens, but I tended to just stay put.

The first couple of nights food was brought in but it was very disappointing. Apparently, my male US coworkers ordered a lot of KFC when they were there, so that is what they brought me. At that time, I guess there weren't a lot of restaurants in that area, so my options were limited. One night they ordered their famous local chicken biryani. It is especially popular during Ramadan and is often used to break their fast. It was delicious but it was a lot of rice which made me sleepy. At some point, I moved to ordering food from the hotel restaurant and taking it to work with me.

I tried asking my Level 3s what there was to do around the hotel, but they kept warning me to "stay at the hotel". In Cebu, the hotel was attached to a mall so I could go out and look around. There was a mall about two blocks away from my hotel in India so on Saturday I decided to go for a walk. I had all weekend to myself, so I wanted to explore a little. I got directions from the front desk. Super easy, turn left outside the gate and walk two blocks.

The area right outside the hotel was mostly run-down buildings to the right and on the left was some sort of body of water/liquid that smelled so bad that I could only spend 15 minutes by the pool. It stung my nose so bad I stopped going to the pool. I had to walk by it, but I couldn't see much because it was surrounded by a fence. The next block was more buildings but not much of a sidewalk. I had to walk over lots of debris, and holes and around cars. As I was crossing the next intersection a motorcycle came whipping around the corner and hit me. I was lucky that I had heard it and then saw him in time to get mostly out of the way. I was hit in the hip/thigh with the mirror which caused me to fall down. It wasn't super painful, but I was pissed that the guy didn't stop or even wave to say he was sorry.

I decided to press on to the mall. It was probably around 10 am at this point. I could tell it was still early-ish because there weren't that many cars on the road and it was fairly quiet. Like in the Philippines, Indian drivers speak to other drivers using their horns. I had to wear my headphones to bed to sleep through all the honking. I got to the intersection and ran across it because there were no lights or crosswalks. There were 3 lanes going in one direction that they would turn into 6 during the busy parts of the day. Driving rules? No, more like guidelines.

I made it to the mall but unfortunately, I was too early. It was officially open, but I could tell most of the shops were closed. I decided to walk around and wait. I had all day and night. In hindsight, I think it was mostly closed due to Ramadan. I do a lap around the first floor and as I cross over to the escalator I slip and fall right on my ass. This was the 2nd time falling on my ass in the same hour! I shake it off, get up, and explore the next two floors but I am in so much pain I decided to leave.

Unfortunately, my nightmare is not over. I could barely walk let alone run so I couldn't cross the street. Enough time had passed and the streets were now packed with honking cars. I decided that I wanted a ride, so I tried to hire a rickshaw. It was too intimidating. The men were gathered around talking and I couldn't get their attention, so I walked a little further to find a taxi, which I couldn't find. I walked back to the intersection, took a deep breath, and ran across the street. Needless to say, I didn't try walking anywhere after that adventure.

I went back to the hotel to rest but as I passed the front desk, I picked up a brochure about taking a tour around the city. As long as someone else was driving I thought it would be safe, so I signed up.

Hyderabad is a large city that is a mixture of the old and the new. The tour I signed up for was a tour of the old including the Golconda Fort, Charminar, the Chowmahalla Palace, and the Qutb Shahi Tombs. It was just the driver and me with no real timeline but also no "tour guide". At the fort, I hired a tour guide from a line of raggedy-looking boys/ men of all ages. The driver left me with the tour guide, and I was a little uncomfortable at first, but the guide turned out to be knowledgeable and entertaining. It had turned out to be a pretty hot day so at some point during the tour I stopped to buy water. I offered one to the guide, but he reminded me that it was Ramadan, and he was fasting. This was news to me. I knew about fasting from food, but I wasn't aware that they fasted from water as well. I immediately felt bad for having both the guide and the driver in the heat but then again at least they were getting paid to be in the heat.

The fort was incredible, the guide showed me how water was stored and moved around, how the king could speak from the top of the mountain and be heard all over, and I am sure other cool things that I can't remember. It was when we went to Charminar that things got a little scary. Scary is probably a harsh word, very uncomfortable is probably better but realistically it was both. Charminar is both a structure and a market next to a mosque. We first climbed the stairs to get to the top of the Charminar which is when I noticed that the driver did not care about my comfort or safety. Many people would approach me asking for money, but he wouldn't say anything. In the Philippines, my colleagues or drivers would shoo them off. Not this guy. It got worse when we were in the market. The beggars would not only come up to me and beg but they would touch me, pull on my arm, and push their babies at me. It was incredibly sad. I had never seen such a thing in real life. I managed to not get into trouble at the market walking but once we were back in the car to go to the Palace, the crowd surrounded us, banged on the car, and even started shaking it at some point. The driver was yelling at them and even hit a few people (with his hands, not the car) which made it even scarier. Eventually, they parted and we made it to the Palace, but I was a little shaken up.

Since you had to pay to get in the Chowmahalla Palace it was less stressful. It was absolutely beautiful, made of white marble with stunning glass chandeliers in most rooms. One of my favorite parts was the carriages. It was interesting to see the evolution from horse-drawn carriages to automobiles. The next stop was the Qutb Shahi Tombs, which are the Indian equivalent of the Egyptian pyramids. Ginormous tombs where kings are buried, well six kings and one queen.

Overall, besides a few uncomfortable moments, it was a great tour. I enjoyed learning more about Hyderabad and its rich history, but it was in the interaction with the people that I learned the most.

69

∾

The Real Life Doogie Howser

My second week in Hyderabad was eventful but not as eventful as the one before. This time I didn't even leave the hotel. One morning after work, I was eating breakfast/dinner and reading a book when an older man sitting at the next table asked me where I was from. I answered "California" and that I was there for work. I asked him and his wife, where they were from and they answered "Augusta, Georgia". They were both professors at a university. I then asked, "Are you here for a wedding?" and the wife replied, "No, we're here to find our son a wife". To be honest, I didn't know how to respond to that, but I am sure responded with something like, "How's that going?" They then explained they had interviews set up for the next couple of days and how they had been to other places in India as well.

We didn't get a chance to talk much longer because they left to start their day. I would run into them periodically when I was leaving for work in the evenings. She would always be dressed in a beautiful Sari, and I would compliment her and ask how things were going. She would say things like, "Beautiful girls", "Intelligent girls" etc. but we didn't get into too many details.

One afternoon I couldn't sleep so I decided to go to the bar to get a drink. Yes, it is still Ramadan but since it was a hotel, they offered drinks.

While I was reading my book at the bar the husband sat next to me and ordered a drink as well. I asked how the search was going and he looked crestfallen. He says all of the women are beautiful, all of them have at least a master's degree and come from well-respected families. So, what's the problem? He said, "The parents." He listed a few things, but one reason was that the parents didn't want their daughters going to America on a fiancé visa. They wanted them to go as a wife. If you know anything about US Visas - a wife Visa is harder. It could take a year or more.

At this point, the wife comes over and they start describing their son and showing me pictures. He is the real-life Doogie Howser. They showed me pictures of him at age 12 winning the World's Science Fair and meeting Bill Clinton. Then they showed me his many graduation pictures. High school at 11, college (NYU) at 13, and medical school at 17. I think there was a picture of him with Desmond Tutu as well. WOW! I was impressed with his story, but the pictures were horrible!! Super nerdy kid with thick glasses and unruly hair. There wasn't a single recent picture of him. Deep down I thought that the pictures were the real reason no one wanted to marry him.

I was curious though, so I asked where he was currently and the husband said, "Why? Do you want to marry him?" then he quickly added, "No, you're too old". Too old??? I was 32 and I looked 24! After I shook that comment off, I was wondering if he was around to meet the women. They replied that he had invented some eye surgery and was currently in India somewhere volunteering. I thought that was awesome, but I was still curious as to what he looked like.

I enjoyed being a tiny part of that experience. Years later, I Googled "Youngest Doctor" and sure enough there is a Wikipedia article about him. I'm sure his parents wrote it for him, and it still has an unflattering picture of him.

70

⌇

Almost Dying in Two Countries
Part 2

After two weeks in Hyderabad, it was time to go home with a quick stop in Dubai. I had a direct flight to Dubai that arrived around 6 am or so. As we were landing, we saw the sun rising over the tarmac. The inside of the airport was like an indoor Beverly Hills. The walking sidewalk is lined with tall palm trees, the building is white marble and gold. Designer Brand shops were everywhere. Once again, I felt a little out of my element but this time because I felt too poor to be there.

This is the part where I messed up. Mistake 1 - I was so used to having "drivers" assigned to me that I forgot to order a driver for myself. Mistake 2 - I didn't do much research on the hotel. I got so used to people making decisions for me that I didn't think to do it for myself. Luckily though, there were plenty of taxis and there were signs everywhere saying that the taxis were safe and monitored. I was exhausted from the overnight flight, so I just jumped in a cab and hoped to get there in one piece.

The drive was less scary than the ones in PI and India. No weird stops, it was daylight and there weren't a lot of decaying abandoned buildings. Instead, there was a lot of construction. Including my hotel. It was new, so the taxi driver didn't know where it was. Smartphones and Google

Maps were still new around this time, remember? The driver had to pull over and use his flip phone to call the station to get directions. No one there could help him so he started driving to the mall that housed the indoor skiing ramp so I could wait at Starbucks. The phone number for the hotel either wasn't working, or no one was answering. The poor driver was as frustrated as I was but just as we entered the mall's parking lot, someone called him with directions.

It was only a couple blocks away and on a new street. So new, only half the street was complete. The other was a mix of sand and mud and that was the half where the hotel was. The driver could only get so close, so I had to walk down a ditch or something and across the street. Once again, I felt dirty and gross and all I wanted to do was take a shower and brush my teeth. Of course, I arrived super early, way before check-in but they were kind enough to check me in and give me a room.

The room looked more like a mini studio apartment. Full kitchen, queen-sized bed, and a full gorgeous bathroom. I was there for only 24 hours, but I would have liked to have stayed there longer. I took a quick shower and then attempted to log on to the WIFI which doesn't work. As I mentioned, I was terrible about telling my family when I was traveling but with the invention of Facebook, I could post where I was and what I was doing. I decided to head to breakfast and then go to the pool. Breakfast was good, the waiter was from the Philippines, so we chatted about his life in Dubai and where else he wanted to go. Before I headed to the pool, I went to the front desk to check out the travel brochures.

Pro Tip / Hack - I Google "Top Things to Do in 24 hours in XXX" before visiting a city/country. Yes, it is mostly touristy stuff but if you only have a few hours in a place you will want to hit all the major spots. Most of the time, there are a lot of museums on the list, but I usually skip those. In Dubai, one of the top things to do was watch the sunset over the sand dunes. I wanted to do this! I love sun sets and over massive sand dunes would certainly be a first. They had a few tours, but one called "Arabian Nights" stood out to me. It included 4 wheeling in the dunes, sandboarding, watching the sunset, shopping (because isn't there always?), and then dinner with Arabian dancers. Sign me up!!

I was staying at a medium-sized hotel. Maybe 12 floors? If I remember correctly the pool was on the 7th floor but outside. It was covered and had an amazing view. I could see the mall and the ski ramp. I could also see the Burj Khalifa, which when finished the next year would be the tallest building in the world. I hung out at the pool for a while but when it got up to 127 deg F even being in the water wasn't refreshing. I was still on my wonky schedule, so I went to take a nap before my adventure. Once in my room, I tried again to connect to WIFI, but I couldn't, not even from the hallway. I was too tired to care though so I went to sleep.

I woke up just in time for the tour. They were picking me up from the hotel, so I just had to change clothes and head downstairs to meet them. I didn't have time to eat which turned out to be a good thing. I am picked up in a Toyota 4Runner I think. A 3-row SUV and it was already full, so I had to crawl into the backseat. Mistake 3 of this trip so far. It is all couples and at first, everyone is pretty quiet. Normally I am chatty Cathy, but I think I was still waking up. After about 30mins we get to the start of the dunes. I thought we were going to change vehicles and get into sand buggies or 4-wheelers or something but no, we stayed in the SUV.

We switched drivers and waited for identical SUVs to pull in around us. After a while, we were on our way. I don't know what I expected but it wasn't what happened. The dunes weren't the sand dunes you see by the beach. They are 10s of feet high. First, you feel like you are going to fall backward climbing up the dune, then you are falling frontwards, then sideways, all the time bouncing around the seats. It was amazing but scary as fuck. I was praying the whole time, "Please don't let me die out here in the sand. No one knows I am here. I will die and no one will claim me". I don't know how those vehicles did it, there were probably 20 of them, all following each other, up, down, and around but no one slid down the dune, no one crashed, and no one died.

We bounced around for about 30 to 45 to fucking forever mins before we veered away from the crowd and stop at the top of a dune. Finally! The part I was dreaming about. It was absolutely gorgeous and the sand was red!! Not white or yellow but red! I took off my shoes and walked around in the sand while watching the sun drop. We still had about

30mins before sun set so the drivers took out snowboards. I had NO intention of doing this but after seeing everyone else take a turn, I wanted to do it. I think it was my competitive side that took over. (Mistake # 4.) Everyone had fallen but it was a race to see who could stay up the longest. For some unknown fucking reason, I thought it would be me. Well turns out I did stay up the longest but unlike everyone else who fell on their ass, I fell face first. WTF!!! Have you seen the size of my ass? Even then about 50lbs lighter - I was all ass! Knowing the laws of gravity, I assumed that my center of gravity was in my ass and I would fall on said ass. Well apparently, not, instead I fall face first and damn near broke my neck! Not only am I now in a great deal amount of pain but I must climb back up that fucking dune!

What was I thinking? I don't ski or snowboard, mostly because I don't like cold but really Daisie? This was a good idea? Yeah, no.

I eventually got up the dune just as the sun was setting and took some cool pictures. After a few, though, I got into the SUV where one of the other guests gave me some ibuprofen. I had sand EVERYWHERE! I tried to shake it off before I got in the SUV, but I was still finding sand when I got back to the U.S.

The ride back was less scary but just as bouncy which made my neck and head hurt even worse. When we stopped for the "shopping" part of the trip I think I walked around for a while but felt dizzy, so I went back to the SUV.

The Arabian Night dinner was another great surprise. (Note: it probably would have been even greater if I hadn't just about killed myself) It was located a little off the highway and had several large tents surrounding a stage in the center. Each of the tents held an activity like hookah, henna, trying on a burka, camel riding (outside the tents), and more. It seemed like we were one of the last groups to arrive AND I was in so much pain I didn't participate in those activities. I went to the restroom and tried to clean up as best as I could. I was able to clean the sand off my face but again - sand for days!!

The seating around the stage was long low tables where you sat on brightly colored rugs and pillows. Dubai, the city itself reminded me of what New York City would have been like in the early 1900s. Lots of construction, noise, and dust everywhere. Where we were now felt more real, more authentic, even if it was for tourists.

After a few minutes, our table was called for dinner. OMG! The choices! So many veggies, salads, and kebabs. I had chicken, beef, and camel! Everything was bursting with flavor! One of the best meals I had had on that trip. While we were eating, the dancing started! I can't remember the names of the dances except for Belly Dancing, which was extraordinary in person. I know there are places you can see it in the US, but I never had, and seeing it there felt so much cooler! The fluidity and sensuality of the movements really were breathtaking.

There was another dance that really stood out because it was done by a man who had a lot of clothes on. Meaning he was dressed in more traditional robes, but the robes were larger and denser than normal. Turns out this is because the robes were used in the dance, like the Mexican and Filipino folk dances with their skirts, he used his clothes to tell the story. He was spinning so fast that the robe would lift to his waist. At some point, he even turned on mini LEDs in them to make the dance even more magical.

If I remember correctly, I think there was even a sword swallower and someone who danced with fire. I think I was in so much pain that I can't remember as much as I would like. It was an absolutely amazing experience, but I wish I hadn't been so careless. I was really lucky that I didn't severely damage my neck in the fall.

71

∽

Walking Like an Egyptian

I returned to Hyderabad a couple of weeks later. This time in a different Taj Hotel that thankfully didn't stink. I also had company, Marcella! She'd been to India several times, so she knew the better hotels, restaurants, craft markets, etc.... Overall, it was a different experience because I knew what I was walking into this time, and I was with someone who knew the place and the people.

Toward the end of the trip, we took the Team Leads, Level 3s, and management out to dinner. It was a mixed crowd and we decided to go to a restaurant that served alcohol. It was still Ramadan, but it was after dark (it was November) so the team could eat. Unfortunately, when we started to order drinks, we were told that we could not since the next day was an election day. Nevertheless, we had a great time eating and talking. Another reminder to always eat with my teams.

I spent a week and a half in India before heading to Cairo, Egypt. I flew Emeritus Airlines again and when preparing for the trip I researched where they flew from Dubai. I found that I could fly to Cairo for $100 so again I was like - "Sign me up"! Going to Egypt was definitely on my travel list. I had always been fascinated with pyramids, ancient ruins, Egyptian gods, hieroglyphics, and of course - Africa. So far, I had only been to Asia, Europe, and Australia. All I was missing was Africa and South America, so this was my chance to check that box.

I had been hearing stories about a system called "Couch Surfing" and was excited to try it on this trip. What better way to get to know a place than by staying with locals? Essentially, "Couch Surfing" is an on-line community where you can find places to stay OR a community to hook up with when traveling. In most cases, it is free to stay there but it is expected to bring a gift, cook, or buy the host(s) dinner and clean up after yourselves. As part of the community, you can be a traveler, a host, or even a community member/leader. Not everyone can host travelers in their homes, but they can host events or meetups.

I read the reviews of several hosts and found one that had an extra room (instead of just a couch or matt on the floor), lived in the heart of Cairo, and had great reviews. I reached out to him and booked his place for 5 days. (Thanksgiving weekend in the US). In preparation for meeting him, I bought gifts of snacks and candies from the Bay Area. I brought See's Candies, Ghirardelli Chocolate, Pistachios, and Jelly Belly jellybeans. Unfortunately, the security in India stole some of the items but the host seemed happy with the treats.

The host, Ali, picked me up from the airport, which was incredibly kind because as you remember, for me, that can be the trickiest part of traveling. It is mid-afternoon but I am once again on a wonky schedule, so we get something to eat and take a nap in preparation for the evening. As it turns out I was just in time for a wedding! An Egyptian man (Couch Surfer host) and a Russian woman (Couch Sufer) were getting married that day and we were invited to the reception!

Talk about an experience I NEVER would have had if I hadn't con-nected with this organization. We were seated with other couch surfer hosts/leaders, and I had an amazing time getting to know them. Egypt, as you know, is an Islamic country but one of the major differences I saw between Hyderabad and Cairo was how the women dressed. They were once again completely covered but they didn't wear the long full black robes. Instead, they wore colored Hijabs (head scarves) and normal clothes. Sometimes a very sexy top but it would have a long-sleeved shirt underneath. I liked seeing the colors, styles, and stamps of individuality they wore. Now, don't get me wrong, there were still women in Burqas but not as many and they would be in different colors.

I don't know if I have mentioned this before, but I learn how to say thank you in every language of the countries I visit. It was at this table where I learned "Shakran". It reminded me of "Sugar" so it has stuck. Like "Thank You" in Filipino is "Salamat" which reminds me of "Salami". (And Mabuhay reminds me of "My Booty".)

After an amazing meal, the party really started. They had dancers from both cultures including many of the same dances I saw in Dubai, including the twirling robes dance. Seeing the Russian dances in person was also pretty awesome and I am glad I got to see it in real life (vs TV) because Russia is NOT on my list of places to travel. After the more traditional folk dancing, there was contemporary dancing. I had an amazing time, and I was excited to see what other exciting adventures the group had planned for us.

72

⌣

Oops I Did it Again

After the wedding, we headed back to Ali's place. I was exhausted so I went to my room and passed out. Turns out Ali was an artist and a night owl, so he stayed up most of the night and slept during the day. The next day, while he was sleeping, I went out to explore a little. What I saw shocked me! All over the streets, people were butchering chickens and goats. I watched several people shave the goat heads. There were feathers, goat hair, and blood everywhere and I was walking around in flip-flops! Turns out I arrived in Egypt just in time for Eid, the celebration of the end of Ramadan fasting. They were preparing for Eid meals, and it makes sense that if everyone lived in apartments - you wouldn't butcher a goat or chicken in your apartment.

That afternoon, Ali took me to a park. I don't remember the name of it, but it was quite large, and I had a view of the Citadel AND the pyramids of Giza (very very faint). Ali didn't look very Egyptian, he had greenish-blue eyes and curly blondish hair, so walking with him around the park garnered a lot of attention. Boys freshly dressed in new clothes and tennis shoes would wave, blow me kisses and call out "Welcome to Cairo" or "Welcome to Egypt". Girls would come up to me and give me hugs, and kisses, and want to take pictures with me. I felt like a movie star. It was unreal and I couldn't help wondering what good I could do if I lived there and learned their language. I was keeping in touch with the women I had met in Japan, Taiwan, and the Philippines, but they all spoke English. Could I learn Arabic?

Soon after the park, we met up with the other couch surfers including two Turkish women for a boat ride on the Nile! Yes, you read that correctly!! This wasn't a large tourist dinner cruise; this was a ride in a small Felucca boat. The nice thing about hanging out with locals is that you pay the local prices. I think for 8 of us, we paid about $2 each. I am sure that if I had booked it myself - it would have easily been $50 to $100. It was past sunset, so this was just a cruise down the Nile at night. Unfortunately for me, most of the group were smokers. After a while, I started to get a headache from the smoke, so I went to the other side of the boat and was joined by Mohammad. He was the President (or something similar) of the Cairo couch surfers, and he had planned most of the outings. He was "hosting" the Turkish girls by making plans, but they didn't stay with him. He worked for an American University or something so his English was exceptional, and he was crazy curious, so we spent most of the ride on the other side of the boat talking since he didn't smoke either.

It was a great experience that I didn't even know I needed to do! Unlike Nagasaki, Hyderabad, Dubai, and Singapore, I didn't Google the top things to do in Cairo. I trusted the Couch Surfers would entertain us.

For someone with street smarts, I can be really naive. A single woman staying with a single man in a Muslim country was probably not the best idea. Again, I don't see myself as beautiful, so I am often shocked when I hear that someone is attracted to me. I was even more shocked when I got in the middle of Ali and Mohammad.

The next day, when Ali was sleeping, I once again went on a walkabout. The one thing that everyone had told me that I needed to get in Cairo was pure oil blends. I must have Googled a shop because I wasn't staying in a uber-touristy area so there weren't tourist gift shops everywhere. I walked into the shop, and not only did it have oils, but it also had paintings on "papyrus" (what they used for paper). I probably spent an hour or more in the shop determining which oils and paintings I wanted. I negotiated with the shop owner and thought I did well when I spent under $200 for six oils and three paintings. I walked around a little more and then returned to the apartment. When I got back, I was proud of my purchases and showed Ali what I purchased. When he asked how much I paid, he went ballistic! He said, I paid too much, and we were going to go to the store and get my money back. I tried to protest because I was ok with that amount. What I bought had value to me, but he insisted so we went back to the store, and he renegotiated with the shop owner. I ended up getting $100 back. I was grateful but also embarrassed. I didn't like his attitude. I was a tourist - I expected to spend money. I had a budget and hell; I wasn't paying for a room, so I had even more money to spend. It was awkward, to say the least, but the day got worse.

Later that evening the group is planning on going to an American bar if I remember correctly. It was one of the few places in the city that served alcohol. One of the guys had a car so he picked us all up. It was crowded and I remember having to cover my nose anytime I was in a car in Cairo. The air quality was horrible, it smelled like gasoline, smog, and exhaust. The cars were mostly older, and they had no regulations. It had also been very overcast, so it was keeping all those smells close to the ground.

The bar was crowded, and you were allowed to smoke inside. Once again, I broke away from the group at some point to get away from the smoke and Mohammad followed me. We talked for a while and then danced for a while, and we had a good time. We may have even kissed on the dance floor, he was attractive and hell, I was a tourist, if I wanted to make out with locals - I could! It didn't seem like a big deal to me. I was only here for a few more days and Ali hadn't hit on me or flirted with me. I really didn't think about it until we went out to eat afterward.

I remember it was a fast-food restaurant named "Queen" something and reminded me a little of Dairy Queen, but it served gyros. It was delicious and it hit the spot after drinking and dancing. If I couldn't have tacos, then this was a perfect 2nd choice. I was so into my food that I didn't notice Ali and Mohammad glaring at each other. Then they started talking heatedly and it got louder and more aggressive until Mohammad left, slamming the door behind him. I was like, "WTF just happened?" Ali told me that he didn't want Mohammad to take advantage of me.

What? Why not? I am a tourist! Hell don't white girls have reputations? Isn't that what everyone thinks we do anyway? To be honest, besides a little kissing in France, I had never really made out with anyone on my travels. In Asia, I was pretty much ignored and in Europe and Australia - I was with my church group. I was flabbergasted but Ali was my host, so I let it go (at least for the night).

Mohammad and I emailed each other and decided to meet at the Egyptian Museum while Ali was sleeping the day away. As I mentioned, I don't really enjoy museums, I would have rather gone to the pyramids but this one housed a lot of the treasures found in the pyramids, so I agreed. It was extraordinary! There was a lot of history and timelines that I didn't understand but isn't that the point? It makes you curious enough to research it more!

It was a wonderful day that felt secretive and exciting. Sneaking away to meet a boy. LOL, it was 2009 and I was 33! I went back to the apartment but managed to avoid Ali. Through email, I told him I was meeting someone for dinner (Mohammad) and asked if we could go to the Giza pyramids the next day since it was my last day. Dinner with Mohammad was at his apartment with his father. It was a little weird. Was he interested in more than a fling? Did he expect me to keep in touch? Take him back to the US? I knew that wasn't what I wanted so I just went with it. Dinner was delicious and the apartment was beautiful. His dad was very hospitable, funny, and just as curious about the US.

Afterward, Mohammad wanted to walk around more (and probably make out) but I started feeling bad. My stomach was cramping, and I felt like I was going to burst. Was it something I ate or drank? I had been so lucky over the years that I think I grew complacent. I got back to Ali's apartment (after leaving my phone in the taxi) and passed out. I woke up the next morning still feeling terrible, but I was determined to see the pyramids!

Giza is about 30 minutes or so outside of Cairo and is a big city. Pictures of the pyramids are taken from a very deliberate angle, if taken from a different angle you would see the pyramids bordered on one side by modern buildings. Luckily again, since I was with a local, we paid local prices to get into the complex. I was so excited to be there, but I felt like absolute shit. It was hard for me to walk; my head hurt and I was nauseous. I did my best to manage because I was in awe. I was looking at 3000-year-old structures, built by slaves for ancient kings. You could feel the mystery, pain, suffering, power, history... all at once. It was overwhelming and magnificent. Once again, I was speechless. How do I explain all these feelings? Even now as I try to put the feelings into words I can't do it justice. All this and I hadn't even been to the Sphinx yet.

Between the pyramids and the Sphinx was a ship. It was buried/pre-served along with a king, and it really was a piece of art and engineering genius. Imagine building a boat to convey hundreds of people without using nails! It was truly amazing but almost immediately after seeing the ship I threw up. Can you imagine? Here I was, experiencing a dream come true and defacing it (not really, I threw up in a trash can). Still, I powered on... I had one more item to check off.

Well, two. I never had "ride a camel" on my list of things to do but when in Giza! Again, Ali negotiated a ridiculously cheap price of having my picture taken on a camel with a pyramid in the background. I wasn't nervous about the camel; I was more nervous about my stomach, but I felt better after throwing up. The camel was lying down when I got on and like on TV they rise slowly, one leg at a time. It was a little jostling, but not too bad. We took a couple of pictures, and we were off.

Every time I think of the Sphinx, I think of E, my college boyfriend. He was a member of Alpha Phi Alpha (APhiA), the first black Greek fraternity. He pledged during the summer before my junior year, and I was part of the whole process (at least in the background). I remember hearing his chants so often that I could recite them and do the moves. The Sphinx is one of the symbols/images associated with APhiA and there-fore when I was standing in front of the great ancient Sphinx, I thought of him and my other Alpha friends, including Brother George.

Again, I can't find the words to express the feelings I had looking at and exploring the tunnels around the Sphinx. My heart is beating fast as I type this. I was only associated with the Alphas and I didn't know the significance of the Sphinx to the Alphas but I still had strong emotions running through me. What would E feel? Would he or any of my Alpha friends make this journey to connect to something so important to their frat? Did Martin Luther King visit? Nothing in the years to come would ever move me as deeply as the pyramids and the Sphinx did except maybe visiting the Martin Luther King Memorial in Washington DC.

I was so overwhelmed with emotions and feelings that I knew it was time to go. I still didn't feel good so when we got back to the apartment I passed out until it was time to go to the airport.

It probably was something I ate or drank. After a miserable flight to Dubai and then to SFO and numerous trips to the bathroom, I felt better. It was such a shame that the two coolest amazing things I had ever done in my life (Arabian Nights and the Pyramids) I didn't get to enjoy to the fullest because I didn't feel good.

73

⌇

Foresight?

Remember my 80/20 rule? I agree that no one can be happy 100% of the time, so I am determined to be happy 80% of the time and when I am not, I try to reflect on where my unhappiness is coming from, determine if it is temporary or not and what I can do to change it. At this time in my life, I am still in graduate school, obviously traveling a lot and loving that part of my job but I am struggling with my job. There had been some management changes and once again - a man who would have never hired me was my boss.

Palm, the little engine that could, was falling behind and management was getting nervous. Google launched the Android just a month or two before our Verizon launch and they were killing us in Marketing. They had a ton of money and it showed. The phone was amazing, and it was all the in-store salespeople would talk about. We may have been the better phone, and it was more affordable but if your salespeople owned an Android - they pushed the Android because they knew it better than the Palm Pre.

You could definitely feel the tension in the air at work and everyone was nervous. It was also a recession. The housing market had crashed, and I was affected by it. The house that I paid $525,000 for was now worth only $250,000 on a good day. I wanted to find a new job but there wasn't much out there. A friend encouraged me to apply for a Youth Minister position but even with roommates, I wouldn't have been able to pay my mortgage. I felt stuck but I still had a job.

I was supposed to go back to Hyderabad, but I asked not to go due to some rebellion that was going on in the city/state at the time. The local people were not happy with the elections. They were blowing up and hijacking buses of commuters and other disorderly conduct. The local team and I didn't think it was safe for me to be there and I agreed. I already glow in the dark, I didn't need to paint a target on my forehead.

Instead, I went back to the Philippines which made me happy. I loved it there! I had kept in touch with the call center manager, Irene, and she was planning an excursion for us. I was excited but I was also feeling pretty blue about everything going on. I got to the airport two hours early as required but the flight was delayed so I went to the food court to hang out and read.

Once again, I was sitting alone reading a book (Sony e-book reader by this point) drinking a glass of wine when a woman asked to join me. A lot of flights were delayed and there weren't any empty tables. At times like this, it really did feel like I had "Talk to Me" written on my forehead. She sat down with her glass of wine, and we spent the next three hours drinking, talking, and laughing.

We both vented about our jobs but also talked about how we coped with it. For me, it had been working with Life Teen and the church but since starting grad school and all the traveling, I had taken a step back. Still, I shared some of my stories with her and she with me. Her current passion project was being the chapter leader for Room to Read, a non-profit that builds schools and libraries in developing countries. I was blown away by her description! So much so, when she left to catch her flight to Guatemala (where she was helping to build a library), I looked up their website and fell in love.

They had a position open for a Cambodia Country manager that I would have loved. In hindsight, I was not qualified for it, but at the time I thought I was the perfect candidate. I loved the idea of Cambodia, and I was a natural leader. Who wouldn't want me? I did apply for the position even though one of the requirements was to have "lived in for-eign country" for two years. I assumed that my travel experience would be enough.

When I arrived in the Philippines, I wrote the most passionate cover letter I had ever written and applied for the position. I never got a response to my application but the idea of Room to Read and living/working Internationally had found a permanent position in my brain.

74

~∾~

Chocolate Hills and Tarsiers

This time in the Philippines was more stressful, this wasn't a pre-launch training. This was after-launch support. Call volume was high, bugs were being found and customers were struggling to set up the phone. The nights were long, and the days were short. The same was true for Irene, she was ultimately responsible for the entire floor. She has been working long hours for months so when she asked if I wanted to get away for the weekend, I jumped at it!

She arranged for us to go to Bohol for a day tour of the island and then rented us a room in a small hotel on the beach. This sounded like a dream, and it was! If you ever get a chance to go to the Philippines, I highly recommend Bohol! It is a two-hour ferry ride away from Cebu.

I am not sure what a day trip would include today but then it started with a trip to the Blood Pact memorial spot. It commemorates the pact between the Spanish and the Filipinos. It was pretty cool, but not as much as the next stop which was the Chocolate Hills. They are called Chocolate Hills because in the summer (not the rainy season) they are brown and look like Chocolate Kisses. I have never seen anything like this. Thousands of ginormous Chocolate Kisses, formed by corrosion, wind, and rain. Absolutely gorgeous and an example of God's, gods', Mother Nature's, or a Higher Power's work.

From there we went to a butterfly farm where I encountered a butterfly that smells like chocolate and one that plays dead. This was my first butterfly farm, and it was delightful seeing all the different species, learning more about them and even watching some of them come out of their cocoon/chrysalis.

When the Palm Pre was first introduced it had some photos/backgrounds already installed on the phone. One of the photos was of a Tarsier, a tiny, adorable primate with huge eyes! I am not sure if that photo was on the phone because of Palm's connection to the Philippines but from the first time I saw it on the phone, I had wanted to see one in real life and my chance came that afternoon in Bohol. Our last stop of the tour was at a roadside zoo-type place. Along with the cutest ever Tarsiers, they had monkeys that stole my glasses, snakes, and birds native to Bohol. Many of them including the Tarsiers, are endangered. A reminder that there is always a cost to progress.

The really cool thing about being with Irene, a local, was that we got local treatment and prices (again). At the time I was there it wasn't overly developed, and it was possible to just show up and still get a hotel room in one of the small hotels on a beach. The original one we stopped at was full but the driver we had hired knew of another one and it turned out to be newer and nicer than the one she had originally wanted.

After a full day of touring around the island, we were ready for some downtime so we changed into our bathing suits and waded in the crystal-clear warm water to wash off the day. It felt amazing to float in the water with the sun starting to lower behind us. One of the hotel attendants brought us some bread to feed to the fish which freaked Irene out. I still chuckle to myself when I remember the look on her face as the fish came swarming to her when she dropped the bread right in front of herself.

It had been a great day, followed by a sunset dinner and an early night. The next day it was back to the city and work. I visited Cebu one other time and that time we were supposed to go to Boracay but there was some issue so instead we went to an amazing resort outside of Cebu City. She rented us a cabana that sat on cliffs overlooking the sea. It was a little bit of a hike to reach the beach, but both the beach and the cabana were worth it. We got that room for about $100, but I remember looking it up online later and it would have cost me at least $400 if I had booked it.

I am forever grateful to my friend Irene for showing me some of the most beautiful places on the planet. I would not have experienced anything like that on my own. I wouldn't have even thought to investigate Bohol or a resort outside of Cebu City. I would have been happy reading a book beside the pool at the Marriot or maybe heading back to the Shangri-la if I was feeling adventurous.

Did Irene do this for everyone? No, she didn't. Most of my colleagues were men, remember? She couldn't take them on weekend adventures. That would raise an eyebrow! Marcella and Kathy were older than Irene and I so maybe she didn't feel as comfortable with them. Regardless, I was blessed to spend that time with her learning more about the Philippines, her, and her family. We were both the oldest in our family and that shaped the women we had become. We talked about our careers and our future. Neither of us was happy with our jobs but what was next?

75

~

Families You Choose

One of my roommates and friends at this time was named Lupita. I had met her and her sister at church. We had gone to both Europe and Australia together and were good friends. She was also from a huge family, and I was happy to be a part of their chaos. Hell, when I lived in San Jose, I was proud to say that I had many families. I would tell people I was part Black, Mexican, and Filipino. I would get strange looks because the only way I could be any whiter was if I had blond hair and blue eyes. I was blessed to be adopted by many mamas/families. My family was still all in Kansas City, Lawrence, or Arizona. Just like when I was younger, these amazing families welcomed me into their lives and homes.

My work BFF, Tim played in a Blues Band with his dad, Jim the "Blues Man" Curry. I would hang out with his mom, Mama Curry, while they performed, either at his sister Deb's house or at a bar/club somewhere. She would introduce me as her daughter, and I really felt like her daughter. The same with Lupita's family, Teresa and Mama Linda, Tiara's parents, and many others. The first time Cristella's dad called me "mija" in church, I cried. At this point, I had a tolerable relationship with my mother. She was still drinking. Everyone but Stephan was an adult, and he was in high school so he could take care of himself.

Moving to CA, helped our relationship. I wasn't able to enable her as much and since I owned such an expensive house, I couldn't give her too much money. I was still paying the mortgage of my house in AZ, but she was paying most of the bills. Of course, that was the theory, but in reality, I was giving her about $1000 a month. Kids and houses are expensive, and she couldn't do it by herself. To my family, I was a bank. They all resented me for one thing or another and even though I loved them, I didn't feel like I belonged or appreciated. Only used.

It was with my chosen families, that I felt like I belonged, appreciated, and loved. Where I wasn't asked for money and then called a bitch. Where I wasn't reminded of every sin and flaw I had. Where I could go to a BBQ and not be on the defensive immediately. That isn't to say that these families were perfect. They all had their own drama, but I wasn't a part of it, so I just enjoyed my time with them.

76

～

Re-Zeroing My Life

It was Lupita who reminded me of the Peace Corps. When I was younger it had been referenced in several movies including "Dirty Dancing" but never in a million years did I think I would join. Me volunteer? For FREE? Yeah no! I had two mortgages, a family to take care of, and a gazillion other reasons. When Pita was talking about applying I remember thinking, "That's amazing but there is no way I could do that." I barely had any savings; I was still helping my mom and I didn't feel the call.

Fast forward a couple of years... Palm gets sold to HP and all my stock is sold. Stock which had split the year or so before. It wasn't a ton of money, but I threw it all into savings. Around this time, I visited Egypt, and I thought about what it would be like to live there and work with the girls. It was also when I discovered the work Room to Read did including their Girl's Education program. I wasn't as involved in my church as I had been, but I still wanted to be. I wanted to work as a youth minister or some type of work that gave back to the world / the community, but I couldn't because I couldn't afford to.

I was living in fear then. If I lose my job, I lose my house. If I lose my job, I can't help my mom. Well, then I decided I didn't want to live in fear. I short-sold my house. What did I have to lose? I was tired of living in fear.

I rented another place, continued grad school, and started planning my next adventure which included the Peace Corps. The Peace Corps came up several times over the years in discussions with the many people I would meet during my travels, and I always had an excuse not to join, but now I didn't. I had enough savings to help my mom for two years, I was graduating grad school soon and I no longer had a house. Why not?

I wanted to re-zero my life. Ever since graduating from college, I had been living paycheck to paycheck. Rent, student loans, credit cards, mortgages, car payments, etc.... I made a lot of money, but I was spending it. If I was making $100, I was living at the $95 level. I wanted to learn how to live more simply. If I made $100, I wanted to live at the $25 level. Where better to learn this than the Peace Corps?

Don't get me wrong, I didn't want to be poor again, I just wanted to make better choices and not get sucked into the world of appearances and expectations. I didn't want to live in fear anymore.

The process to join the Peace Corps is a long one. You apply, wait, interview, wait, take a physical, and then wait some more assuming you make it that far. I remember being asked in the interview where I wanted to go. Deep down, I wanted to go to Africa but then again, how cool would Vietnam be? Or Samoa? I couldn't decide so I answered, "I know where I don't want to go."

The interviewer said, "Oh yeah where's that?"

I answered, "Central Europe."

"Why is that?" he asked.

"Because they look like me," I replied.

Sometimes being the only white person in a crowd can be uncomfortable but the times I am uncomfortable is when I am learning and growing the most. I don't always get it right, I don't always say the right thing the first time, and I don't always understand but I always try. Everyone has something to teach you.

My travels have shown me that all humans have the same desires and those are to love and be loved and to take care of those that they call family. Everyone I have met throughout my misadventures has been proud of their city/state/country and they wanted to share it and their experiences with me.

Joining the Peace Corps was an opportunity to not only re-zero my life but also experience life in a foreign country as a member of the community and not as a tourist. White people in foreign countries are not a new strange thing but a white woman traveling by herself in many countries is. It draws the curious and the brave alike. The people I have encountered wanted to learn more about me and why I was traveling there as well as share their experiences. That is the mission of the Peace Corps; to learn about your community so you can share it with your US friends and family, and to share your experiences living in the US with your new community.

77

~

An Earthquake and a Hurricane

I will share the many craisie misadventures while in the Peace Corps sometime in the future, but in the meantime, I want to share an adventure that is a perfect example of what you can encounter if you open yourself up to it.

My mother's birthday is a few days after mine, and she had gotten into traveling for her birthday like I do. She was going to meet me in Hawaii for my 33rd birthday but that didn't work out. She visited me in Mexico for our birthdays in 2012 and then the next year she visited my brother Sean and me in San Francisco. In 2014 she was turning 60 so I decided I wanted to do something really special. Initially, I wanted to go to Brazil but after some weird cancelations, we booked a trip to Jamaica to celebrate my 38th birthday and mom's 60th.

Since my mom lived in Arizona, I decided to book our flights from there. My friend Miguelle would meet us in Jamacia since she was flying out of SFO. I got to Arizona a couple of days early so I could hang out with the family. The day before the trip I was on Wikitravel looking up things to do in the area we were staying when I read, "Americans do not need a Visa for Jamaica." FUCK!!! No, but they need a fucking Passport! At 4:00 in the afternoon the day before my trip I realized that for the first time in my traveling career, I Daisie, Queen of checking boxes, Miss Perfect, left her passport in CA!

I was flipping out; I called my brother Sean to help me out, but he was taking a nap, so he was all bitchy and moody. I called UPS and FedEx, and no one would deliver the next day (Sunday). I looked up flights and the next flight was $700. I woke up Mom from a nap to see if I had left my Peace Corps passport there (no), we thought about driving to CA but Sean wouldn't meet us halfway and we didn't want to spend the next 24 hours in a car driving so we decided to send Stephan. I was so mad at Sean that I didn't want to fly back so we sent my brother instead so he could hang out with Sean and then come back the next day.

At 5:30ish I booked the ticket on SWA that departed at 6:50 and they left the house at 6:00. They got to the airport at 6:05 and he made the flight. He sent pictures of an empty flight, him posing with the flight attendants and the free alcoholic drinks he got for being my hero. He had a layover in Vegas, so he sent more pics from there with the slot machines.

Mom and I were beyond tense at this point, so we started drinking and repeating over and over, "It's only money!"

So far, the trip hadn't started so well, and I woke up the next morning paranoid. I texted Stephan to make sure he found the passport. Through-out the morning Mom and I texted him repeatedly asking him where the passport was, does he have it, etc.... I am sure he was very annoyed, but he was a good sport about it.

As we were texting him, we found out that he had just survived a huge earthquake in Napa. There wasn't any damage to where he was staying but they did feel it and it shook us all. I was so grateful that nothing had happened to either of my brothers. Can you imagine if Stephan had been hurt because I had forgotten my passport?

Luckily, he made it back on time and in one piece, so Mom and I headed out for our big adventure.

If I had put all my faith in signs, I might have canceled this trip. First, I forgot my passport, then the earthquake, and after checking in our luggage, I tripped and broke my flip-flop going up the escalator. I had no other shoes on me, and all the stores were closed but luckily mom had an extra pair on her. She had tiny feet so they barely fit, but they worked for getting through the airport and during the flight.

Turns out Miguelle was having similar problems on her way to Jamaica. She hadn't realized she had such a long layover over in Atlanta and wasn't happy about sleeping in the airport. Mom and I had a short two-hour layover in Miami, but it was six o'clock in the morning and all we wanted to do was sleep. We did have just enough time for her to take a smoke break and for me to buy some ridiculously expensive flip-flops.

The flight to Jamaica was smooth and we were glad when we landed and were on our way to the hotel. As we approached though it was getting darker and darker. The clouds were rolling in and just as we arrived it started pouring! Turns out there was a hurricane in progress on the other side of the island. We had no clue. Mom and I checked into our room, called Miguelle, took naps, and then met her for dinner. Back home Maisie was worried about us and was trying to get a hold of us, but we didn't have WIFI or phone service. The rain came and went over the week, but we never realized how close to a hurricane we were until we got home.

78

∾

Doing What I Do

Part of the reason I am writing this book is because I have been encouraged to do so for years by friends after hearing one of my craisie stories. They are all true, to my memory, and only slightly exaggerated and I love telling stories and sharing my adventures. I never really know what my family thinks of my stories though. Family, meaning my brothers, sisters, mom, and uncle. Many of my stories were told while we were sitting out on the patio eating BBQ, drinking, and hanging out. There is some part of me that thinks that every time I start talking, they roll their eyes and say, "There goes Daisie making shit up again." Who knows what they think, it doesn't really matter because my mom got to witness me in action.

The day after we arrived in Jamaica, we decided to explore the city after breakfast. I had chosen a hotel right downtown in Ocho Rios, literally around the corner from the main part of the city, shopping, and restaurants. We hit the local Mercado first, where locals in stalls try to sell you the same thing. I had been to a gazillion of these, so I knew not only to haggle but to go to the stalls in the back because they give you the best deal. This is because most tourists don't go all the way back there. Not only will you get good deals, but you will see more of the real people. Oftentimes, it is women with babies at their breasts, old men and women with no teeth who call you their beautiful friend, or young girls and boys watching one stall while their parents are at another. It's crazy and beautiful at the same time and my mom loved it. We bought all kinds of little stuff for the family.

Miguelle was also used to this, but she had a different philosophy than we had. We bought stuff before we spent our money on other things, but Miguelle would just shop and shop and shop. We had a bag full of stuff, but she didn't buy any of the touristy stuff in the market. She had mentioned that she was looking for a jumpsuit-type outfit or a long dress, so we headed to the actual shops next. There were probably only about 10 shops and they offered everything from shoes to women's clothes to water sports equipment. We mostly window-shopped because it was still early, but Miguelle saw a dress she liked in one window, so we decided to check out the store.

When we got to the door it swung open and two women greeted us, and immediately you could tell they were having a ball. It was probably between 10:00 and 11:00 in the morning and they were just chatting away and their mood was contagious. We started with the normal pleas- antries. Where are you from etc.... It's funny though because there are now 5 women in this little clothing shop all talking at once so you have to repeat yourself when someone asks again. We said we were from CA/ Arizona and one woman replied to me that she was from New York but was from Jamaica originally and was visiting home.

I said, "That's great, is there a special occasion?"

She replied, "Yes, for my birthday on Saturday."

I laughed and said, "My birthday is tomorrow, and my mom's birth- day is on Sunday."

She looked at me funny and asked "Sunday?"

"Yes," I replied.

She laughed a great big laugh and said, "Mine is on Sunday too but my party is on Saturday."

So of course, I bring my mom over and I say, "My mom will be 60 on Sunday."

The lady laughs again, gives us big hugs, and says that she is turning 60 as well on Sunday!

OMG! How wonderful! What a small world!

She proceeded to invite us to her party and really encouraged us to go. She tells us all about the food and how her family and friends from all over will be there etc.... We don't have any set plans and this is the kind of adventure I like getting into so we agree!

79

~

Yah Mon!

In case you are wondering, they really do say this! Besides being close to the downtown area, one of the best parts about the hotel was the service and the guests. The hotel was filled with people from all over the world including several Jamaicans on vacation from other parts of the island or the US. The staff was extremely courteous, helpful, and full of yah mons! I personally liked all the eye candy. I probably would have brought back a husband or two if I wasn't with my mom. Hell, who am I kidding? She was encouraging them to flirt with me! Not that I minded but after a few days I was tired of the flirting and just wanted to read. I wasn't Stella, my groove was just fine, and I wasn't bringing back a husband.

For most of the trip Miguelle, Mom, and I would meet for breakfast and then do our own thing for most of the day. For me, that meant finding a great place on the beach to read and beat off my many admirers. Mom would join me for a while, get antsy, and then go swimming or snorkeling. Miguelle would go off on different adventures into town. Little did I know that one of those adventures was looking for a pineapple upside-down cake for my birthday per Mom's recommendation.

Although I can read every day and still get into trouble, we also decided to go on a few adventures. The first was the Dunn's River Falls. I had no clue what we were getting ourselves into. I thought it would be a short hike to the falls then people played in the water and looked at the falls. This is not the case; it was a hike up the falls! With my almost 60-year-old mother, who had had back problems the last couple of years. I was so afraid that when they asked us to line up, I made sure I was right next to her and almost fought the sexy young man who was the guide. Turns out he was going to be her partner and ensure she got up safely. My mom loved this! Not only did she get to hold his hand, but he also flirted like crazy with her and made her laugh. It wasn't an easy climb either, it was on smooth rocks that had been covered by moss, but the guides scraped the moss off every morning. Regardless, it was slippery, and it was hard to watch my mom and myself so I was glad she had her new boyfriend with her.

The guides were great, they carried our cameras, took pictures, and had us cheering for each other and laughing a lot. There were a few more adventurous activities on the way up the falls and my mother was braver than me and did both. One was a natural slide which I did do but the other was falling backwards into the water and mom was first in line!

80

Swimming with Dolphins

Unlike most of my other traveling adventures, I was pretty broke during this trip. I wasn't making the money I used to make before my Peace Corps days, I just spent $700 to get my passport and there was someone to consider besides myself. Mom and Miguelle wanted to swim with Dolphins and although I had done it before who was I to tell my mom no? If I had known she was going to die less than 6 months later, I would have done even more! "It's only money".

My mom was a fish! She would take us swimming as kids, and she often talked about swimming in high school, but I don't think it dawned on me how much my mom loved to swim until we went on this vacation. She was always in the water and not near the shore wading around. No, she would swim so far out that I would lose track of her. She would show up later describing where she went and what she saw.

We swam with dolphins the day before her 60th birthday which was also the day of the party we were invited to. When I swam with dolphins in Mexico it was in a huge pool and there were only two dolphins. In Jamaica, it was in the ocean, and I think they mentioned they had like six dolphins. They broke us into groups, gave us life jackets and we swam into the ocean. This freaked Miguelle out! She must have thought we were going to be in a pool as well and was almost hyperventilating as we swam out to our part of the cove. Mom, on the other hand, was bursting with joy. She was smiling and first in line for all of the activities. We were given several opportunities to pet and caress the dolphins, take pictures with them, and swim with them. We had a blast and of course, we had to buy a couple of pictures to remember the moment. The picture of the dolphin kissing my mom was the picture we put on her funeral program. Her smile was the brightest I had seen in a long time, and I was glad that I helped put that smile on her face.

81

〜

Happy 60th Birthday!

While we were swimming with dolphins, the lady that was hosting the party called and left us a message at the hotel saying that the party venue had changed. I was touched that they went to the trouble of informing us of the change. It meant they really wanted us there. We rested and then got ready. We hailed a cab not realizing it was about a 20–30-minute ride. We weren't the last to arrive, but we certainly weren't the first. When we arrived, we found that they had set us up with our own table in the front and just to the left of the main table. The lady who owned the shop joined the table with us and we settled in.

The birthday girl made her entrance a few minutes later on a throne being carried in by four men! She was wearing a gown that I would call a "quinceanera gown" full of silvery colors that sparkled in the light. She looked marvelous! So happy and proud of her moment. Once they lowered her to the ground, she did the most amazing thing, she thanked everyone for coming to celebrate her and Mary Helen's birthday! Right from the start she involved my mother! It was one of the most beautiful and selfless things I have ever seen. My mom was so thrilled I thought her face might explode she smiled so wide. I can still picture how happy she was as she stood up and let the other birthday girl introduce her to her friends and family.

After the grand entrance and a few short speeches, we were sent to the other room to grab food. It included all of the Jamaican favorites, jerk chicken, goat curry, plantains, and more. After dinner, we danced for hours. It was an amazing experience and I am glad I got to share it with my mom. See - talking to strangers doesn't always get me into trouble!

The taxi driver hung out at the party with us, so he was able to give us a ride back to the hotel and only charged us for one way. He was so sweet to my mom, and it was a perfect way to end the perfect night.

82

∾

To Be Continued

I started writing this book in 2014 after a Mexican beach trip in Ixtapa for Christmas and New Year's. I was probably ⅔ of the way done when my mom was admitted to the hospital and then died a few weeks later in January 2015. Luckily, all of us kids were able to see her before she passed. Sean, Stephan, and I drove from San Francisco and Maisie flew in from Lawrence during MLK weekend. I spent her final weekend by her side in the hospital and left 12 hours before she died. As I was leaving, I asked her if she wanted me to stay. She was being released to in-home hospice care. Her last words to me were "No, go build libraries."

I had started my dream job three days before she was admitted to the hospital. I was the Applications and Project Manager for Room to Read, the nonprofit I learned about in the airport that had started my journey to the Peace Corps. I was so excited to help bring books and education to children in developing countries. Losing my mom devastated me so I did what she asked and threw myself into work. Unfortunately, I didn't have the energy or mind space to continue with the book. I brought it out a couple of times and did some editing, but I don't think I added too many new chapters.

You would think that COVID would have been the time to finish this book and you are partially correct. By March 2020 I was working as a consultant, and I did have some free time but I still wasn't ready to go there again. COVID was hard at first with all the fear and insecurity around it. My company was already remote, but they soon changed their structure and I got busier.

In January 2022, I met a woman named Rosalie who would eventually proofread the first draft of this book while we were on COVID quarantine. I have many stories to share about my travels with Room to Read and personally. I haven't had as many near-death experiences (you do learn more with age) but I have met many amazing people while sitting at a bar or table reading a book. I want to share them all, but I also want to get this book out! Yesterday, I spent hours re-reading and editing the work I had already done and then I wrote a couple of new chapters. Today I have been writing and editing for over six hours now.

Why do I mention this? Well, I seem to have found my mojo again! This, my dear readers, is not the end. My story will continue! I have been living the digital nomad life since COVID and have spent time in Mexico, Oregon, Chicago, Florida, South Carolina, New Orleans (currently), and Europe.

Thank you for joining me on this journey and I look forward to sharing more with you!

Acknowledgments

I want to first thank - you – the readers! Many of you know me personally and probably picked up the book to see if you were in it. LOL! Well, I hope I did you and your story justice. If I didn't, I apologize or maybe you are in Book 2 (Peace Corps) or Book 3 (Post Peace Corps). For reals though, thank you for being a part of my life. Every single person who has come into and out of my life has made me who I am today and I am blessed!

A HUGE THANK YOU to readers who took a chance on a random travel memoir from a non-famous person. I hope you enjoyed my craisie stories and they encouraged you to travel more.

To my BFFs, Tim and Tiara, thank you for your constant love, support, and encouragement over the years. I wouldn't have joined and then survived the Peace Corps without you. And yes, you will be in books two and three!

To my new sisters, my Erika, Addie, and Elery - thank you for welcoming me into your family and loving me through everything. You aren't in this book because I wasn't blessed with you yet, but you were with me throughout the journey of writing the book. Claire, thank you for the AWESOME book cover!! I LOVE IT and can't wait to see what you do for the next two. Emily, thank you for your encouragement and the color you bring to my life. Lisa, thank you for being the reason I came back to St. Petersburg and finding "Home" again. Erika, Addie, and Elery - thank you for being family. I love our errand days!

To Amelia, Paul, and Pam, for listening to my stories and encouraging me to write this book! I loved our times together in Mexico!

To my ladies, Rosalie, Linda, and Julie, thank you for your love and support over the last three years. You are all AMAZING women, and I am blessed to know you and have you in my life. There will definitely be several misadventures that star the three of you in book three! Along with our harem leader – Dan!

To my ORTEGOONs – everything I do is for you and everywhere I go I take you with me. I can't wait to have misadventures with you one day. I love you Josie, Ernie, Buddee, and Mari. You are my heart and soul and I am blessed to be your Auntie.

To Aimee, fellow Dragon, almost Virgo, and lover of Key! Thank you for everything!

To Uncle Jim, Thank you for being the father I didn't have for so many years, thank you for always supporting everything I do, thank you for being my next-to-biggest cheerleader. I wish Mom could have both of our books. She was certainly a part of the journey for both of us!

About the Author

What more could you possibly want to know? You just read a whole book about her!

Criaisedaze is Daisie Hobson in real life. Currently, she is a consultant and digital nomad living/working wherever she feels like. She LOVES reading, traveling, and working with her amazing clients.

If you enjoyed this book and hope to see more please leave a review wherever you purchased this book.